The Tea Leaf Reader

The Tea Leaf Reader

Sarita Gupta

Master of Science, Computer Science

Bachelor of Engineering, Electrical Engineering

ISBN: 9781073559541

Published in June 2019.

Imprint: Independently published

Publisher: Amazon LLC

DEDICATION

To the alchemists, atheists, agnostics and the devout.

To the humanity-haters and the benefactors of humanity.

To the left-brained and to the seers.

To the "star-crossed" and to the privileged.

PREFACE

E very truth in Physics are applicable to practical life situations of people whether it occurs within the body or in our actions and reactions with the outside world.

I started writing a book more than a year ago, in April 2018. What I wanted for my first book has changed over time. This book kept growing beyond 300 pages with a new book getting created with a different title. So, I have about twenty-one book titles in my files to be released in the future. But the first book I suppose always takes time because of the extensive thought going into what should and should not be in it, especially when it is supposed to introduce you to people.

I was then told that I cannot release my first book until I am a crone. I was told that I could publish bits and pieces of my book and wait for a few years to publish the rest.

PROLOGUE

People see a book on Metaphysics or on Energy Healing on the shelf and dismiss them thinking, "Yeeah .... another person rambling about the existence of god and pseudoscience and asking us to meditate." Even worse when we see a book on Ascension practices, we think people who couldn't achieve in life are trying to settle down for less and teaching people to follow non-violence. But the truth is that our minds cannot fathom or comprehend what we do not know. We need to know to fathom or debate about that subject. Authors are philanthropists extending people's horizon beyond their unknown. Even if a book is lying, it forces the reader to think and search for the truth and learn.

I realized that if I do not include some chapters on the mechanics of our spiritual self, people won't have a full understanding of how the spiritual problems afflicting us fan out within and without, including the news that I am trying to disseminate about the invisible problems facing us.

Writing about Metaphysics with certainty requires knowing the ultimate truth, that mortals, even big monarchal queens and kings, Shamans, and sorcerers may not know of, for which I have searched to find knowledge from the Collective Consciousness and have made use of my clairaudience to obtain the utmost truth from the divine.

Intuition is a scientific conclusion derived via a short cut. Intuition comes from the Infinite Intelligence which we sometimes refer to as the Divine. The intuitive method arrives at the solution much quicker, deriving it using the complete picture of the entire possibilities of cause and effect. Sometimes intuition provides a more accurate solution to a problem for which we may use Science to arrive at an approximation of it. The difference between intuition and the derivation of resulting conclusion from available facts, is that the available "facts" to us may not be accurate and all facts may not be available, so it is good to connect with the Collective Consciousness in search of the truth to find the bottom line. These days I rely more upon my intuition, which is non-inferential knowledge from claircognitive downloads that pop into our minds. I also use my clairaudience to talk to star people, to verify facts.

This book reveals some of the deeper secrets of our existence that no one talks about, because they want the book to make money, or they don't want to be shunned by friends, and came to be popular. It reveals some of the darker and uncomfortable secrets of life that we choose to sweep under the rug, finding comfort in ignorance as bliss. Such information is scattered throughout the book in the form of accounts and anecdotes.

The buzzwords, such as star attunement, raising frequency of bodies, taking Earth to a higher dimension, ascension, meditation, and spirituality, were all started and funded by the star people from the star people, some behind the scenes and some that were lost in History. The following words are borrowed from the language of the stars: Shaman, Akashik records, Avatar which is the reincarnated self,   Cosmic   which is used in universal or cosmic consciousness, Harmnik (convergence), Tantrik, Droom which is used in drumming into transient states of the mind which enables us to receive healing from realms outside of the human reality, Psyke which is used in Psychology, and Telihk which is telekenesis, and Okkul for occult.

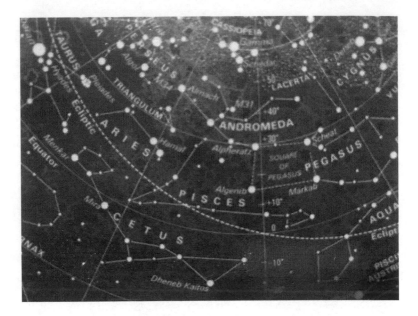

Photo: @1982 George Philip and Son, Ltd, Britain.

The above photo shows the Cetus galaxy. It is quite far and outside the Milky Way galaxy.

For the spiritually savvy, who are familiar with the metaphysical buzzwords and the popular interpretation of some of the spiritual inklings that exist among us, this book is neither a redefinition of it, nor an account from my own experiential spirituality but throws light on the truth about some of the spiritual concepts and the origins of how they came to be known. It takes people years to get a sense of the unknown.

Eight years ago, I had bought the Dragon NaturallySpeaking speech recognition software, to write books. I think, I thought, that I had too much of my life's learnings to share with people, so that people could learn from other people's mistakes, life and strife. I never took it out of its box. I suppose, we don't venture out of our comfort zones unless we are pushed beyond our limits of normal cognizance and our tenets of comprehension. When people hit a wall within the known, whether it is their fault or other people's, it doesn't matter, they try to search for the truth in the unknown.

CONTENTS

INTRODUCTION

Scientists discuss if life exists outside Earth. It does. Not just on Mars but outside the Solar System too. This is as true as it gets, even though we have a lot of media ridiculing alien encounters and UFO sightings. People do get contacted by star people in their dreams and also in waking consciousness if they have clairaudience. The star-wars aren't all lies either and a handful of us do end up interacting with the Space aliens, especially during times of war. The eleven movies on star-wars that have made about 180 million dollars each weren't conjured out of thin air.

There have been many books in the last thirty years on star people but none of them came from a left brained person who has a Bachelor's degree in Electrical Engineering as well as a Master's degree in Computer Science from a name University such as Vanderbilt in Nashville, Tennessee, and has worked as a software engineer for sixteen years. The book shares and explains the paranormal as well as life problems with a scientific approach.

Star people do affect our lives in invisible ways that result in visible problems in our bodies and in the climate, the roots of which, we haven't correlated to the goodness and the havoc brought down from the stars.

I want people to think and learn about the deeper secrets of life and nature, the truths about our existence, who we are, where we are headed to and such.

The book shares some Metaphysical truths and some of the invisible happenings in and around Earth drawing our attention to some of the burning problems affecting us, along with some suggested remedies to minimize negativity and bring positivity into our lives and on this planet.

I want to throw light on alternative methods of healing and share some of the good and the bad about them. I don't mean the Voodoo doll tricks or the Wicca spell casting but knowhow about our own existence.

We experience our spiritual selves and the invisible realms of Earth more than we know in our cognitive reality or waking consciousness.

CHAPTER I

THE UNKOWN

SPIRITUAL AGNOSIA IS BY DESIGN

I ronically, some of the contents of this book are known sub-consciously to about ten percent of humanity from their dreams and trance states, of which they do not remember after coming out of it, so humans know much more than they recognize in their waking consciousness.

I wasn't going to write about spirituality, given even Pharaohs who were real kings and queens never taught spirituality to people and only did genetic work for us and built some temples and pyramids to funnel down relic power from Sirius to sustain Earth and protected Earth from the earth-hater star nations. The biggest monument left behind by the Pharaohs, the Great Pyramid is not a tomb. It is a precise eight-sided prism with relics at specific points to vortex down power from the Sun and radiate out in specified angles to most of the land mass, the Nile valley being the central location on the map of the World. Each of the four sides have a middle line making each side two straight plates concaving in at an angle of about 4.6 degrees each. It was a scientific structure which was used by people who would go inside it and stand at the center, to connect to star people and receive claircognitive downloads into their heads and is also a relic in brick and mortar which was keeping diseases away from the area. The Great Pyramid was designed by star people from the Hathor civilization and the Sun. Even as early as ~7800 years ago, people used to go inside a pyramid to talk to star people though these were limited to the Pharaohs, the high priests, the chief architect and the chief physicians.

"Seeing is believing" was taught to us when we were made spiritually agnostic 300,000 years ago after Earth was severely attacked by the star people. Then our spiritual powers, clairvoyance and clairaudience were taken away so that we could ignore the attackers and the uncontrolled mob conjecture could die down and we could live. However, in the last two years, many star kings and queens wanted us to know who they are and be more cognizant of the invisible happenings in and around Earth, so that we could be politically educated and act with accountability in the event we get abducted by star people. However, now in the aftermath of the recent star-wars targeting Earth and the subsequent crises created because of curiosity killing the cat, and humanity getting too much rope to figure out, it is now desired that humans not have clairaudience and clairvoyance except for a chosen few.

My physical self in the human waking reality never believed in spirits, ghost sightings, or even the existence of star people until my clairaudience and clairvoyance fully opened up in May, 2014. People who talk about paranormal activities or UFO sightings, get strongly dismissed by people as delirious.

There are a few people that I know of, who have had their awakening of their extra sensory perception commonly known as clairvoyance, clairaudience, clairsentience, claircognizance, and such, and when they start hearing or seeing spiritually, various people start showing up including those from the stars and most of them are there to harass and so people go through a whirlwind of paranormal experiences. When they speak about those experiences to their relatives and friends, they are suspected to be mentally ill or even schizophrenic. Some even get sent to mental health facilities on the grounds of expressing "delusional beliefs" in public. Some were also sent by their own families to behavioral health care facilities when found that they could be talking to "themselves". The reality about us getting chipped by star people is true. I know of someone who when asked for an x-ray at a hospital to find the location of suspected chips was detained upon the grounds of mental and emotional disorder and shipped to a behavioral correction facility for fourteen days. Then such people get prescribed with Lithium for almost all of their lives and who could have been a person with open chakras who is spiritually gifted with emotional wisdom and higher than average intelligence, gets rendered to someone with impaired memory, poor coordination, mental retardation and confusion. Thereupon, friends and family of these people learn from their experiences that clairaudience is bad for them and that any "seeing" will be considered hallucinating with subsequent hospitalization with loss of job and prestige, so they shun spiritual growth and think that Earth is all that exists, and that star people obviously do not exist.

The star people and the supernaturals of Earth are not visible to us because their vertices or coordinates of existence are different than ours. The purpose of this separation has been to sandbox civilizations that did not want to interact with other civilizations, to stay separate in their existence and interactions. This was a conscious political decision by the star people who are the benefactors of Earth.

The sandbox terminology is used in Computer Science to specify an environment in which developers or end-users can create and test new content, separate from other content in the project. The contents of a sandboxed environment do not have access to or interfere with the contents of other sandboxed environments. That is how our phone apps work, where different apps work independently of each other and their data are not shared or accessed across apps. However, we do end up interacting with the space aliens, especially at the times of war when energetic walls made up of laser or Solid-State barriers are broken either as a part of a targeted war strategy or as a side effect of another havoc. Electronic engineers are familiar with what a Solid-State is, but for the layman, it is a state of matter in which materials are not fluid but retain their boundaries without support, the atoms or molecules occupying fixed positions with respect to one another and unable to move freely. Therefore, what we can touch and perceive and feel within the vertices of human reality is sandboxed away from other realities which are thus invisible to us.

Within the sandbox of our human reality, if we had to demonstrate the existence of the invisible people such as the star people and the ghosts, we can, through what is called paranormal activity. Shamans and healers routinely experience this and term it as "phenomena" within the community of the energy healers. These paranormal activities follow the principles of Physics as much as the activities that are considered normal or ordinary activity. For example, when a ghost or a star person moves a piece of paper from point A to point B, the star person has applied a certain force from across the barriers of their own reality which is different than ours. The object moves from point A to point B based upon the reluctant force applied upon it from across the barrier. The actual force imparted from across the barrier is usually much different because a lot of that force goes into breaking through that barrier and in some anecdotal cases a whole power of Saturn was used to break a leather sandal on Earth. Though in their defense they didn't break just a stitch but the piece of leather itself. I want to make a note here that I am using the words 'realm' and 'reality' interchangeably. Coming back to the example of the ghost moving a piece of paper from point A to point B, we call it a phenomenon because the object moves but the mover is invisible. The mover is invisible because the mover is in a realm different than the human reality, sandboxed away from us. The mover exists across the barrier of sandboxing and the force applied upon the object to move it, seeps through a transformation from across the barrier, so, the movement of the piece of paper occurs, but the mover is hidden. Sometimes the kind of force applied upon the object to be moved, from the other side of the sandbox of our reality, may not be mechanical, and could be a different kind of energy coming through a conversion principle. This can occur in the human reality too, like in the case of motors where electrical energy is converted to mechanical energy or in the case of a vehicle which runs on fuel or chemical energy.

A proof-reader had argued:

"We don't see this happening across apps."

"That's why this is called phenomena. Phenomenal!", I had replied.

It is true that data should not being able to move across apps. The seeping of information across the sandboxed apps happen when the hackers successfully hack our computers and the apps. Here the hackers' work of one app such as a Bank App accessing data from another app such as the Contacts App look like magic in the same way when an invisible person moves a piece of paper from point A to point B. I used the word "magic" here because it is a word that is often used exchangeably for "phenomena", which occurs when the sandboxed barrier created by the use of pre-programmed Solid-State devices and laser that keeps us separate from the invisible people, is hacked or broken. Normally people on the other side of the sandboxing should not be able to impart any energy across the walls of the sandboxed environment or world, to move that piece of paper. Yet the hacking happens when star people and other invisible people use their powers that exist for them in their reality to physically move objects in the human reality which isn't normally possible but, is allowed by the law of Physics when the power infiltrating the human three-dimensional realm is able to break through the security measures of our realm. Such powers are usually higher powers than the security locks protecting the invisible container of our reality. The combination of powers that star people use to create the window to access or do things in our human reality, vary and are usually a mix of the Elemental powers of the stars, Elemental powers of Earth, powers of Darkness, and powers of the light or those of the darker light realms.

Star people and other invisible people routinely use their powers that exist for them in their reality to bring physical movements and changes in the human reality. Besides paranormal activity, interactions with the invisible people does leave a mark upon us in the form of "natural" disasters and havoc upon our minds and bodies including plastic surgeries in sleep and other surgeries as a form of attack, where people are left to fate, trying to guess why their skeletal structure changed after a certain point in their lives. Left untouched, we are supposed to grow old, gracefully, and not fall off the limits of facial recognition.

Photo 1. by Sarita Gupta, taken at the Sakya Buddhist Monastery, Dehradun, India.

The Photo 1. depicts the sacred paraphernalia and offerings at the Sakya Buddhist Monastery at Dehradun, India. Many of us rely upon mercy from the darker light lords and the Darkness lords and offer our prayers and keep our fingers crossed. Prayer also allows the more benign light beings and our star benefactors to help and so we do get touched by the divine too.

EXISTENCE OF LIFE OUTSIDE EARTH

I found that about a hundred humans have had interactions with star people that they also remember in their waking consciousness.

Earth is one of the planets where people are kept in a box not allowed to know more than what meets their eyes within the daily treadmill of their lives, herded through a mold of life. The reason for this is political. Not within Earth but in the Outer Space. Yes, life does exist outside Earth and Outer Space aliens do affect our lives at a continuous basis. This is unfortunately hidden from our reality and shows up only as new autoimmune diseases, rising crime rates, astrophysical problems and higher occurrences of seemingly natural disasters.

Almost all of the planetary bodies and stars, and some nebulae, have life forms that look humanoid besides other supernatural creatures and flora and fauna. Some Some of these planets or stars look   like the tropical islands with lush green vegetation and some have big cities like New York, and some have very ornate palaces like bigger versions of the Indian fortresses. Some planetary bodies are covered with water mostly, with bigger oceans and much smaller landmasses. The planets within the Solar System including the Sun have humanoids, supernatural people with tails, the Saurischia and other animals and reptiles that look more like the creatures categorized as extinct or mythical on Earth, such as the flying reptiles, the plumed serpents and the humanoid looking reptilians. The supernatural people with tails are sometimes referred to as monkey-people, but they don't look like monkeys. They look like humans with a tail and are more sinewy with higher physical powers.

After three years of extra-terrestrial interactions and scientific, paranormal investigations I discovered that only people having the spiritual gift of clairvoyance are actually able to see the star people, unless they are in a dream, or a trance-like state induced by the means of self-hypnosis or by the alien trying to interact with them. We can't hear them, but people who have acute intuition with extra-sensory audibility can hear them. People usually don't remember the interaction after the trance has ended, some because the star people involved in it erase it from the memory, some because the parts of us that had the experience were abducted or left for some reason, and some because we don't have a good dream recall circuitry in our brains or it wasn't functional.

I made the discovery that when a human witnesses an UFO (unidentified flying object), they are still seeing it spiritually, the vision of the UFO not being at a hundred percent like one would detect a hot-air-balloon dropping from the sky with the action being initiated within our human reality. The view of the UFOs and other alien objects come through a translation principle due to which it is muted in its intensity because our planet has a protective barrier surrounding itself, therefore the alien objects from on the other side of that encapsulation have to hack through Earth's shield to be detectable or effect our reality after some of their energy is spent in breaking the opposing barrier that protects us from being able to be affected by the UFOs and flying saucers. Star people only effect us through conductors or natural seepage across our barrier, disintegration or decrypting of our barrier to create access doorway, or hacking devices coupled to a transformer, for example, eavesdropper systems, ports, hubs and switches latching onto our atmosphere through a transformation algorithm, even when they are applying lever-action to effect us at a greater magnitude.

We get to view the UFOs when our protective barrier around the Earth has been weakened by the UFO for them to interact within our reality, or the area is a crossroad with thinner barriers, or the UFO people want you to see them for which they have created a window of visibility to interact with us. Humans who have the gift of clairvoyance may see more than what the UFO chooses to show.

Some people mistake local spiritual space boogies to be an UFO or an alien flying object. UFOs are not generated on Earth and come from outside. About seeing stars, we see them with our naked eyes and not clairvoyantly. The view of the stars come with the help of the properties of our atmospheric barrier alone and off course our naked eyes. If a foreign UFO is visible through naked eye, it must have higher intensity for us to see it without us having clairvoyance because when the humans have clairvoyance then they are wearing an invisible lens-like upon or within their eyes, mapping onto a window between the two realities or realms of that of the human which is our regular reality in which we exist and operate and that of the UFO system's sandboxed realm.

The star people or the space aliens as we sometimes refer to them are classified by the spiritual teachers as spirits because their form is etheric, like ghosts of dead people or like soul-parts of living people who are in astral-travel mode outside their human bodies. This mode of wandering around by the living like how the astronauts travel within their space shuttles, is called an out-of-body-experience (OOBE). I want to clarify that when living humans astral travel, they obviously don't float with their whole physical body like the astronauts do, but they do so only with parts of their soul that are loosely attached to their bodies and can move around and come back in. These parts of the soul are etheric and would have the consistency of smoke. When we are astral-traveling we can interact with the ghosts and the star people if we happen to meet them. We do not remember what our soul-parts do while astral-traveling because their heads are not in the physical body's head unless the soul-parts are fully integrated in the body. Thus, we experience our spiritual selves and the invisible realms of Earth more than we know in our cognitive reality or the waking consciousness.

I was once teaching a group of people at a Drumming Circle assembly about the existence of humanoid life outside Earth.

"Then, why didn't we see these people when our astronauts landed on the Moon?" someone enquired.

"This is because the astronauts had the same eyes and powers as they have on Earth, where if the Moon people visited, they wouldn't see them." I replied.

I shared with the group that at the time of the Moon landing, the Sun king was there to ensure safety and to maintain decorum. Eight dinosaurs were gathered there by the order of the then queen of the Hathors. The Saurischia were asked to guard against unforeseen attacks from the Earth-hater nations and to make sure that the astronauts landed safely. The entire Moon landing mission was possible because of the extrat-errestrial stakeholders of Earth and several Light kingdoms. The technicians who wrote the Moon landing code, had received claircognitive downloads from the engineers of the Atmel star. The moon landing was watched by about 20 different galaxies. It had been a novel feat for us since the completion of the Taj Mahal, which is one of the seven wonders of the world. Lately the moon landing project has been considered a waste of resources by several star kings who do not want Earth people to have clairaudience or get out of Earth at all.

As I finished talking to the above group of people, a king's son from the Moon appeared and greeted. I noticed that he looked about 9 feet tall and elongated in stature. I figured that he looked shorter on the Moon. I did not share words with him. I gathered that people look taller when they land on Earth, because of the difference between the gravitational acceleration of their atmosphere and that of Earth's. I had never seen any person before who was stretched taller, not magnified taller but stretched taller. To satisfy my curiosity, I wanted to walk myself through the mechanics of it using the laws of Physics. Then I invented a new Law of Astrophysics as follows: An astral alien's height changes after they land in our atmosphere on Earth according to the difference between the gravitational acceleration on Earth and that on their planetary body or encapsulated realm of a Space ship.

To investigate further, the center of gravity of a body is the hypothetical point where the entire mass of the body is assumed to be concentrated. The Newton's laws of motion work with the center of gravity of objects were the forces of gravitation, for simplification purposes, are always assumed to be applied to the center of gravity.

Representing force at the center of gravity of a body as f, and gravitational acceleration as g,

$f_{\text{on Earth}}$ = mass of the person * $g_{\text{on Earth}}$

$f_{\text{on Moon}}$ = mass of the person * $g_{\text{on Moon}}$

Given the mass of the body remains same, after equating the above 2 equations, $f_{\text{on Earth}} = f_{\text{on Moon}} * (g_{\text{on Earth}} / g_{\text{on Moon}})$

Through my firsthand observations of the changes in height and subsequent calculations, going by statistics and conditional probability, I made inverse inference from data about the underlying process that generated that data and deduced that the gravitational acceleration on the Moon is about 1.5 times higher. Thus,

$f_{\text{on Earth}} = f_{\text{on Moon}} * 0.667$

Thus, the force experienced on the center of gravity of the body is lower on the Earth and is at about two-thirds of what the body is used to experiencing on the Moon. Hence, due to the lower force on the center of gravity of the body, this point rises in height to keep the person on the ground. The distribution of mass is always balanced around the center of gravity, and because the mass is not changing here, the body still looks proportionate but just stretched taller. To bring further clarification, they don't look bigger like in a magnification where you take a photo and then magnify it proportionately 1.5 times, they look as if the photo was stretched 1.5 times only in the height. To explain further, the width of the body of the visitor from the Moon seemed to remain as same as what it may have been on the Moon, due to which the lateral forces on the body seem to be about the same as upon the Moon.

In the year of 1901, the General Conference on Weights and Measures had defined a standard gravitational acceleration for the surface of the Earth at 9.80665 m/s2. My hypothesized approximation for gravitational acceleration on the surface of the Moon is 1.5 * 9.80665 m/s2. Then after further experiments, I standardized the constant of gravity on Moon to be at 15.41 meter per square-second, thereby converting my hypotheses into a new Law of Physics, stating a new Constant of Astrophysics, gMoon for gravity on the Moon with its value being exhibited as follows: gMoon = 15.41 m/s2.

To summarize, a new astro-physics Constant for the gravitational acceleration on the surface of the Moon was invented in this chapter and represented as gMoon to be at the following value:

gMoon = 15.41 m/s^2.

From another experiment where I stood upon a simulated version of the Moon by a process of space travel, where I could touch and investigate the surface of the Moon, I made the following deductions from my observations.

New Law of Physics, Law1: In the concept of a constellation rotational speed is proportational to magmetic pull at the center of the planetary body.

New Law of Physics, Law2: Space objects that have higher magnetic strength in the core need to revolve faster to maintain their orbit in stellar Space.

- For example:-

I. Within the Solar System rotation of a planet needs to be faster when magnetic pull at its center is higher.

II. In inverted systems, created by inverted flow taps, the planetary bodies that have lower magnetic strength in the core need to revolve faster to maintain their position in stellar Space.

New theories discovered in Astrophysics as follows:-

Theory 1 - The Moon's atmosphere is ~ 19,200 meters high.

Theory 2 - The density of the Moon's atmosphere is 10 to 15 times higher than the density of Earth's atmosphere, varying based upon climatic region.

Theory 3 - Physical bodies on the Moon experience approximately same horizontal forces as upon Earth.

Theory 4 - The viscosity of the Moon's atmosphere is higher than the viscosity of Earth's atmosphere.

Photo by CORBIS.

Theory 5 - Physical bodies on the Moon experience roughly 2.26 times higher downward vertical force per square foot than on Earth.

Theory 3 and Theory 5 is the reason it was easier for our astronauts to walk upon the Moon with their Earth physical body. Usually, most of the aliens remain in their spaceship or have ambulatory aid which are inbuilt in their bodysuit with magnets and special magnetic fields and other propellers pre-installed to guide their movement.

Once an astronomer who had been studying the existence of life on Mars, complained to me about not being able to detect life on Mars using the technology available on Earth. He disclosed that he had met Mars people on Earth, inside a Darkness realm and was tortured by them. He said that when he disclosed that to his fiancé, she did not believe it and gave him the cold shoulder. He then added that a month later when he had talked about it with a colleague he was more receptive of the story. I knew about the unrest on Mars and so did not delve into that story and went on to explain that our telescopes see through human eyes created for our own three-dimensional reality. Given we can't see star people without the aid of clairvoyance, we can't see them through the telescopes. Seeing spiritually is like seeing through a lens which is like a window of scientifically allocated portal to be able to view another reality or realm on another plane of vertices. I say vertices instead of coordinates because some planes are spherical or elliptical instead of just cuboidal, and the shapes are limitless. Such seeing is termed as clairvoyance. The way to fully interact with star people is to get out of our bodies and being allowed into the same sandboxed realm as them, because then it would be like being in the same room as them. I then told the astronomer that if he reached Mars astral-traveling via an Out-of-Body-Experience (OOBE) and asked the Martians to allow him to see them and if they allow, he will be able to see them.

STAR-SEED

Star-seed is a term popularized in the last fifteen years to specify someone from star origin who wasn't consigned as a human but has taken birth in a human body. Star-seed means a person of star origin who has had a handful of incarnations on Earth either from the star type of the creators of humanity or of the type of the humanity-haters, for accomplishing big, phenomenal tasks of saving or destroying Earth.

Some star people take human bodies by forcing out the existing human soul and etching themselves in and attaching to the Chakras of the body so that they can function as if the body is their own and live like that for years. These are not defined as star-seeds but act like one. This usually happens in the case of star convicts and vagabonds looking for a place to stay or linger or star people attracted to a human and deciding to marry them or be their consort or star people who are strategically placed in a human body by their government to work against this planet.

However, some star people take the human bodies to do scientific work or philanthropic work.

The star-seeds from nations that support Earth, are the pioneers catapulting major revolutions, like the onset of Bronze Age, Iron Age, the discovery of America, the French revolution, the Industrial Revolution, and the Technological Revolution. They have brought new methods of healing, for example, "Sound healing" and Shamanism which was pioneered by the Hathors, Acupuncture which was pioneered by the Chinese star people, and Reiki which was started by the Koreans.

Many star-seeds have different physical attributes such as skeletal structures that fall outside the range of human specifications such as elongated necks, differently shaped ear lobes and eyes, different retinal properties, and angular or even angelic faces. They usually have issues with human enchantment for frivolity in social situations where people make small talk. At parties they usually observe, not necessarily from a corner but walk around and observe. They usually can read everyone's minds and know who they are in a nutshell and what they are up to. Many people think that they are arrogant or have an off-handed mannerism or are shy. Star-seeds are also very busy within, because they can see and hear more than other humans so they usually keep to themselves and talking to them could be like pulling teeth.

I used to wonder why star people in human bodies are called a star-seed. I found two years ago that this term was coined by someone from the stars, about fifteen years ago. The part of their soul energy that was brought down from the stars to add on to the rest of the zygote when they were being developed into a human mold to be born upon Earth, is a guest upon Earth but not necessarily that soul type because there might be many humans already upon Earth from places in the stars from where pieces of their soul originate. In an anecdotal evidence, the Pleiades government had started commissioning their own and their neighboring people as humans, about 744,000 years ago. Some of these people are a Neanderthal-like race in their genetic makeup and found in modern day Netherlands. They themselves don't take birth upon Earth but take human bodies and fully etch themselves in, to function in human reality and they get etched into those bodies at age twelve. They possess those bodies to help out the people that Pleiades had created on Earth about 12,000 years ago. They work to awaken their consciousness to higher levels of compassion and understanding, to be able to take them back legally as former convicts who have completed their term of suffering and free to live a life in the Pleiades. Some of the people from Pleiades who take human bodies are royalty from Pleiades and they do it to do scientific and astronomical work. For example, I discovered that it is extra-terrestrial technology why the surrounding water in Holland doesn't flow in, even with a higher sea level than the adjoining land. They do have very slight barriers to stop the water from rushing in, but the water chemistry in the bay is engineered and more coagulant. The photograph on the next page shows that if the water was less coagulant the waves would spill over the embankment onto the adjoining land which is lower than sea level.

Photo 1., taken on 7/5/2012, at Marken, Netherlands.

THE INVISIBLE REALMS OF EARTH

Humanity does have unconscious understanding of the invisible realms of Earth, for example, our bed-time stories and fairy tales talk about fairies, angels, druids, elves, trolls, the sasquatch, werewolves, and the sea monsters. The bigger creatures, for example, the dragons and the dinosaurs are mythical creatures with magical powers who live in the invisible realms of Earth which are not part of our human realm, thus we cannot see them with the naked eye. I discovered that being able to see these supernatural beings requires clairvoyance, however we can see them just fine when we are outside our bodies in our etheric form because then we have stepped into their realm. The creatures of the invisible realms of Earth are usually not part of our human realm and so we can't see them with the naked eye. At a particular point in time, when we co-exist in the space co-ordinates as that of the other realms, then we can interact with the people of those realms. Unfortunately, we don't always carry forward the memories of such interactions just like we sometimes forget our regular dreams, though we do retain subconscious memories of such paranormal incidents.

There is a reason we do Space Clearing with the help of priests or shamans at the time of buying a new property or setting up a new shop. The invisible creatures of Earth have their own realms that are hidden away in the woods, rivers, oceans and the mountains, but can occasionally infiltrate the human reality such as our houses and streets. The people conducting Space Clearing, clear the space of home or office from imprints of trauma, unwanted energy, ghosts, unwanted spirits from the invisible realms of Earth, and do general healing of the space. Sometimes dead humans and even Neanderthals are attached to a place for various reasons which need to be addressed with compassion and cleared, if needed. For further information the Neanderthals died collectively about 27,000 years ago and live on Earth in spirit form and sometime possess human bodies in exchange for helping the human with work which are usually engineering work. Most of the Neanderthals who were commissioned to Earth were Engineers and Scientists. They had a space issue and weren't convicts in the stars.

The realms and realities on Earth usually exist independently in its own container having its own axes. One or more realities can hold the same space or partially overlapping space, and not share their coordinates of existence; it is like two or more superimposed cuboids or other kinds of containers. When such realms coexist in the same space, their contents and people normally do not collide or interact with each other but can interact if the security walls are broken down by hacking the individual containers of space. An example would be the trees all of which are part of our human reality but a handful of them also have their own different realms which are superimposed upon the human reality. These trees can perceive and interact with our reality, just like our soul-parts can when they are outside our bodies in astral travel mode and can see and hear according to their individual power levels. The more sacred trees like the sycamore, the Holy basil known in Hindi as Tulsi, the Eucalyptus, the Douglas fir, and the Sandal trees have more powers like the supernaturals of Earth and so they can see more. Some of the powerful trees can see and hear us even when they are stationary and haven't stepped out of their bodies.

Sometimes different realms coexist in the same space, and share their spatial axes, like two containers superimposed in the same space on the axis of time. An example would be two three-dimensional cubes overlapping each other and having the same spacial coordinates with a 4th dimension of time stacking them. In this case people do not collide or interact with each other, unless they share the same token of time. This is done to create time slices of events within a particular space, so you can think of it as a time machine where you hop on and go to the past and hop off and come back to the present all in the same room. This is the medium basic concept of a Time Machine. Another version of the Time Machine would have different vertices but share the same superimposed space, with each container having its own time axis.

Normally, the contents of the other realms cannot be perceived by us using our five senses. As humans we only see in our own 3-dimensional reality and only the very gifted Shamans, Lamas, Star-seeds and the seers can see other realities, but it would be like walking through the coordinates of the other realms like stepping in and out of cubes but can't see them all at once. Only very powerful light-beings can see them all at once.

In Shamanic lore there is a terminology known as the Middle World. The Middle world is the collection of all the realms on Earth and the human reality, whether or not these realms are visible to us.

The supernaturals usually live in the mountains and in the woods and even underneath the surface of the Earth. Some have realms that do not touch Earth but not that far from the surface. There are many supernaturals that co-exist with us everywhere. The Jotuns from Norway live in the woods, the werewolves and the coyotes live in the woods in North America and the Kamis live on the top of the Fujiyama Mountains. The Yetis, and Yakshas live in the Himalayas, the Condors in the Americas, the Centaurs in Greece, the Tuatha de Danann live in the Celtic Otherworld, the plumed serpents in Thailand, Cambodia and Mesopotamia, and the flying lions which are known as the Azghirabhat live in Egypt and ancient Mesopotamia. There are the fairies, the Faye beings, the sprites, the nature-spirits, the druids and many more. The dragons, condors and the plumed serpents still live on Earth even though they are not visible to us. They live in higher dimensional Euclidean realms in different areas of Earth, though these days the newer realms are not Euclidean. Some of the creatures that I named sound extinct. Among the well-known extinct creatures, the ones that are actually extinct from Earth are the mammoths, and the flying fish.

There are settlements inside Mt. Shasta where a lot of supernaturals from the Pacific Northwest live. They forged friendship with the supernaturals living on the Himalayas in the 1960s. Since then some of the Indian demi-gods and supernaturals started living in the invisible realms inside Mt. Shasta. That is the prime reason why in the early 1970s we saw a surge of Indian immigrants buying motels and houses in California. The supernaturals do influence the minds of certain key people who are rich or hold positions which can influence the larger society.

There are two distinct ways for us to experience the invisible realms of Earth. The popularized way is to drum to a certain a binaural beat that can transport the mind onto the theta brainwave level at 6 to 11 Hz. In theta state, our senses are withdrawn from the external physical stimuli and once that layer is dormant, we can connect to our inner, more powerful self of the star person that we are. In human body the powers are reduced and that is why we do not have the "clairs" in our waking consciousness. Once in trance, we can eject from our bodies and transport our bodies to an invisible realm and there we can see, hear or fully interact with the inhabitants, depending upon our powers of hacking through the security gates of that realm. Some people see in shadowy forms, some in grayscale and some in vivid colors. Usually people see and hear better with their eyes closed. This experience is like inducing a dream at will, where one enters the dream state of theta or even a deeper beta brainwave, and hence can detach from one's physical body and cross over a threshold to another room, full of artifacts and creatures where one can interact in another reality. At this point they become part of the other realm where they have entered. We usually do not have both clairaudience and clairvoyance in a trance state, and we do not have the power to enter multiple realms at the same time.

The other way to experience the Middle World reality is to bring a realm to one's location. In the first method one was journeying to a different realm while in this method the realm is coming to you, so it is the opposite of entering a room. In this case you can imagine that a room full of artifacts and creatures are coming to you and overlapping with where you were situated. After this, one need not to be in a trance-like state to be able to see and interact, however the creatures of this other realm may interact with you normally like other humans do in the human waking reality. A safer way to bring a realm to oneself is to still maintain the energetic barrier between the incoming realm and the ordinary human realm and create a window to view and interact with the contents of the other realm. This would be like teleconferencing or videoconferencing where bunch of people from outside the monitor interact with your real-time. They can talk and laugh and share a joke but cannot throw a punch that would actually hit you. For this, one needs to be in a trance-like state to be able to see and interact. This is the state where we have elevated powers to be able to access the windows of interaction. Only a handful of shamans can enter the Middle World reality without drumming into trance. The difference between drumming to another location, versus trying to enter a trance-like state where we are situated would be to hold the intention of not going to another location but to stay put where we are.

Sometimes realms come to us with their own window to interact with us and the creatures of this other realm may interact with us without us knowing about them like how witches put curses upon us, or star people do spiritual surgery upon us.

DREAMS

There are many documented literature on dreams and the interpretation of dreams that speak almost well about deciphering the hidden meaning and the signs that one re-one receives in one's dreams. Nevertheless, I am going to talk about what dreams are, how real they are, if they actually occur, if you have actually interacted with those people in your dreams and why we dream.

The following are new metaphysical facts about dreams.

❖ Dreams are a gift from the divine.

❖ They are not supposed to occur.

❖ Dreams tell the truth.

When people are put through situations and tasks that were not designed for them to handle and they have hit a wall then the divine steps in to help them out of their situations so that they could live and they could handle some of the unforeseen stress and life could move on for them. Dreams are real. All the happenings in the dream actually occur. We don't understand about half of them because the unseen forces of Darkness or enemy "Lightish"-es who have thrown us offboard in the first place to necessitate those kinds of dreams mess with our heads and try to make us believe that those dreams aren't true. Powerful intruders plugged into our heads or even chips from star people enable them and the dark angels to know what we have dreamt and so they specifically put a mask upon our dreams and unfortunately the value of those dreams is lost.

Statistically, on Earth people benefit from their dreams only about twenty percent of the times. This is mostly because we have this innate urge to shun the unseen. Dreams are the closest we have ever come to knowing the spiritual world and interacting with people who are otherwise unavailable. The unknown faces in the dreams are the light-beings who we do not know and the known faces are people who are brought into our dreams by the divine to reveal a critical information to us or walk us through things we do not know and urgently need to know.

Some of the dreams are hard to interpret because whoever had been asked by a higher light to fix a situation for us and doesn't really want to fix shows enough in the dream that the higher light is satisfied but it doesn't help the dreamer. For example, many times in my childhood I have seen dreams of being chased by a bull or being attacked by a bull. I think almost a dozen times. I couldn't make sense of it. I learnt much later that what they wanted to convey is that I am being bullied here and there in the invisible realms of Earth and also in the light kingdoms. Well I learnt the accurate interpretation just now, from the one who had shown those dreams. Back in 2016, I had taken some Energy Healing sessions from a shamanic practitioner who has clairaudience and clairvoyance, and I had asked her to channel the interpretation of that repeat dream and she had lies for me. It is important to receive energy healing only from people who pass your red flag instincts and follow your "gut" and not go after how well they advertise themselves.

I want to bring attention to some of the non-dreams that we take as dreams. These also occur for real and we aren't watching a TV of those incidents. These dream-like occurrences are different in the sense that you can perceive that you are still on your bed and you are interacting with invisible people in your room as if they have visited you. In this case you are in a deep trance and probably talking to a star person or a light-being or someone from Darkness. The other scenario for the non-dreams would be where our soul-part has stepped out of our body and gone astral travelling somewhere to one of the invisible realms and have interacted with people there. The way to tell the non-dreams apart from the dreams are that the dreams are more symbolic. The more real-life the interactions are where there is not much to take away as a learning or an information to something bigger, the more it is just that we have interacted with ghosts, star people or other supernaturals. These interactions usually involve a talk or a fight and are not allegorical.

The best way to interpret our dreams is to keep trying to decipher what we couldn't in the dream and some day the truth would pop up into our heads and then follow through what was told or shown in the dreams. Even though some dreams are cryptic they still tell something which is true.

While I was conducting spiritual research on dreams, in my meditation, a divine being said:

"It is imperative that we abide by our dreams. That is how the divine wants us to choose in situations we aren't prepared enough or informed enough to choose and change our course of action accordingly."

The above is necessary to achieve our full potential and bring lasting positivity into our lives and lives of people around us.

Photo by Sarita Gupta, taken in July 2017, depicting the Sacred Cow on a wall of the Hatshepshuht temple in Luxor, Egypt.

HOLY COW

Certain cultures on Earth worship the cow as sacred. Rig-Vedic, Indian dictionary of verses mention cow worship. This practice started a long time ago, close to half a million years ago when the Indian god Brahma started helping the Hathors in their work of settling Earth. The divine powers of the Hathors that helped with creating the skin of humanity were created and maintained by the clans of the Hathor Cow Supernaturals. About half of the Hathor queens had some portion of the Cow supernatural energy in them. The Hathors worshipped the other supernatural beings too. You will find their images carved on the walls of the Egyptian temples. These were the snakes, the cows, the birds, the lionesses, the alligators, the Scarabs and even frogs. Incidentally, Photo 1. presented on the next page satisfies the inquiry about seeing the relief of a frog being worshipped in an Egyptian temple. It shows the mural of the supernatural king of the Hathor frogs upon a wall of the Abydos temple in Egypt, built by Pharaoh Osiris.

Photo 1., by Sarita Gupta, taken in July 2017.

After the people from Obalesk, Arborra and the other Hathors settled humans in various parts of Earth, a big chunk of today's population was brought from the stars and settled on Earth by Brahma who had struck alliance with the Hathor administration about 70,000 years ago.

The cow worship in India started after Brahma introduced it about 45,000 years ago in Northern India where he was based at that time. The Indian cows that were worshipped were from Keshw. The cows were considered divine because they carried a bigger heart and they could channel divine power and wisdom more easily. Their closeness to evolved consciousness was of the likes of the high priests of other supernatural clans. The cows believe in the goodness of others more easily and quite unceasingly.

Photo 2, taken at the Kailash temple, India

In northern India the bulls are also worshipped. They were brought to Earth from the Indian God Shiva's place in the stars. The Photo 2, shows the Kailash temple where people are worshipping the sacred bull outside the temple.

Humanity has collectively died and re-created many times, for example at the time of Noah's boat, at end of the Atlantean civilization, and even as recently as ~20,000 years ago, over the cycles of which the worship of cows died everywhere else except for in India.

The Hathor cow-people have interacted with me. In the month of August, 2016, I saw one of them in my room in my condominium at the city of Bellevue in the state of Washington, USA. He was roughly seven feet tall and his ears weren't like those of humans, but a hybrid between a cow and a human with more a cow. His face had a bovine impression. From his actions and exasperations, I figured out that he was dragged into my place from the stars and hadn't been upon Earth before arriving at my place of dwelling. I suspected that he belonged to the race of Hathor Supernatural cows and was an ancient being because he appeared as a life-sized, animated rendering of the Hathor Cow-people found in Egyptian literature. He seemed to be in an etheric bubble of an extra-terrestrial realm, which mimicked a mosquito net, with I viewing clairvoyantly, through an interior doorway secured by a curtain of a semi-transparent, fluid panel. He seemed dangerous with his bulk and as he started to dart in my direction I pulled myself out of that trance-net. I learnt much later that the reverie was cast by one of the star rulers of Earth, also using Indian spiritual technique of Mayajaal where "maya" stands for hallucination and "jaal" stands for net. The above figment or figurative segment of time is an example of a non-dream which I have discussed in the chapter, titled as "Dreams". On another occasion in the month of January, 2018, I was in a dream where I was idling away, outdoors at the Hathor Cow planet, which is far from Earth and outside of our Solar System. There I was swinging by a pole when a taller woman with bully demeanor who seemed to be living upon that planet arrived and without talking to me much, she hit me in my jaw. It is hard to talk about what is going on for Earth that isn't visible to humanity. There is a constant star-wars going on since a year and this involves Earth directly. I wish that good people would receive justice sooner than later.

THE HUMANOID FORM

Human bodies are made up of soul that fills up the body, and body materials. The body materials are comprised of the elements of air, water, fire, earth and sacred space. For the computer savvy, if you take the analogy of a human body as an object of a C++ class defining the human species, this "sacred space" is a property of the physical body and carries the instance of the container class of the Earth's three-dimensional realm or space within which the body is permitted to function. This three-dimensional realm defines the sandboxed environment that contains the human reality including us, flora and fauna, our cars, buildings, roads etc. This would map to a pseudocode like the following:

```
class Human
{
private:
```

```
        ....

        // The private property s is for the that realm

        // this human body is contained in.

        static Space _s;


public:

        void Human(Space s);

        void Breathe();

        ..

} // End of class Human


// Constructor for Human

void Human::Human(Space sobj)

{

        .... // Other initializations.

        // When Humans get created the constructor is

        // called by passing the parameter Space-::get().

        // So, each human is tied to the Earth's

        // 3-dimensional space.

        _s = sobj;

        ...
```

```
}


int Human::Breathe()

{

        int alive = 0; // 0 for success

        // Breathe in the atmosphere of Space _s

        // air_comp[O2] is used and other molecules

        //are processed out.

        int result1 = Inhale (_s->air_comp);

        int result2 = Exhale ();

        .... // other computations and calculations for alive.

        return alive;

}


// Earth's 3-dimensional realm.

// In layman terms can think of it as the atmosphere.

// The class is designed to be a Singleton because each

// human need to use the same realm and we do not want

// multiple instances our reality.

class Space

{
```

```
...

private:

        static Space _instance = null;

        int atmos_pressure_to_creat;

        double tilt;

        double rotational_speed;

        Coordinate pos_in_space;

        Vertices size;




    // Private constructor for making it a singleton

        Space (int atmos_pressure_to_creat, double
        tilt, double rotational_speed, Coordinate
        pos_in_space, Vertices size)

        {

                // Code to create the space object...

        }


    // Air composition array being created by passing

    // instances of the molecules of air
```

```
        object[] air_comp = new object[] {O2, CO2, N, Ar,
        OtherMolecules};

            ......

public:

        static Space get() //static getter.

        {

                if (_instance == null)

                {

                        _ instance = new Space (atmos_pres-
                        sure_to_creat, tilt, rotational_speed,
                                    pos_in_space, size);

                }

                return _instance;

        }

        ...

        Vertices Expand (double percentage);

        Vertices Contract (double percentage);

            .....

} // end of class Space


class Vertices

{
```

```
    private:

        int length;

        int breadth;

        int height;

    public:

        void Vertices (int length, int breadth, int height);

            .....

    }
```

/ * In the above pseudocode, the Human object could be packaged to behave like a "Service" process where it breathes automatically at certain intervals and does other involuntary body functioning, and for voluntary tasks, it receives external inputs for which interrupt receiving systems are in place for appropriate action. */

We are a humanoid form where there is a body designed in a certain way and there is a soul. Our souls were brought from the stars and created into our genetic form or species. So, humans originated in the stars and were commissioned out to Earth from their native places, as political refugees or as prisoners of war. Some of us had lost our stars or planets to flooding or explosion or other forms of inhabitability, some of us were captured as prisoners of war by the star nations ruling Earth and some of us were shipped out of our planets or stars due to other political reasons, to a reformatory planet such as Earth. Earth is part of the bigger universe where the planets are designed to serve their stars as revolving objects around them protecting them, and to be used as a home base for their militia or a planet where people work in a give-and-take mode of giving spiritually in return for a better life.

It takes time to digest news that is different from known facts that shape our minds growing up, so it is expected that most of us will find it hard to believe that there could be humanoid life outside Earth and that the universe is big and there are too many stars and planets where people live almost like on Earth. They are people like us who are alive, who have families, houses, money, legal systems and accountabilities.

The aboriginal creatures or supernaturals of Earth are the serpents, the dinosaurs, the fire dragons, some of the Pisces, the flying reptiles, locusts, and the grasshoppers. Among bipedals the only aboriginal supernaturals are some of the Saurischia who can almost walk straight with their forearms in the air. The saurichia of Earth had moved to different planets 300,000 years ago when Earth's dimension was lowered. Some of them came back to Earth in 1979, in anticipation that they would be restored on Earth and continue to have a good habitat here. Due to extensive star-wars since 2010 some of them were relocated to Jupiter and Saturn because their palaces were ruined.

The photo on the previous page shows an aboriginal saurischia of Earth. These creatures actually existed on Earth and looked like this. They have longer neck than other saurischia. This version of the dinosaurs are known as Euhelopus and they do not have wings but can run fast like elephants. I have actually clairvoyantly met one. I cannot capture them on camera because they are invisible within our three-dimensional reality, so I used PowerPoint Graphics.

The Humanoid form of being is not the same as the supernatural form of being which were naturally created by the divine. The supernatural form is like a mono-soul type. By mono-soul, I mean that snake souls are born as snakes, monkey souls as monkeys and bird souls are born as birds. The supernaturals are monkey-people, snakes, alligators, bird-people, serpents, felines, tigers, dinosaurs, other saurischia and so on. These were the original supernaturals, but over time the supernaturals have born with mixed souls whereby they add parts of souls of different creatures into one soul, for example, a monkey supernatural being born with part monkey energy of their own with some soul energy of a snake and some of a bird added on to themselves. This mostly started with royalty who were looking to garner respect for ruling more than one type of supernaturals.

The humanoid form wasn't created by the divine but by the mortals. One such story of how the humanoid race came into being is from 800 billion years ago with the help of Darkness powers derived from torturing female monkeys. These monkeys whose cells had turned into that of darkness, were left with a vestigial form of their original selves, where they didn't have tails and did not have semblance to their original looks. They walked upright like we do and had minimal body mechanics and mechanism as compared to what they used to have in their supernatural forms. They preserved their remaining powers and the leftover scanty cells to be able to fend themselves from future impending attacks. After struggling in a darkness realm for a million years, they were released from that realm and transported to their home where they were somewhat healed by their naturally occuring Elements, which is air, water, fire, earth and space. They were about 2,000 in number and had gotten used to their body. The neighboring places picked up the idea of creating humanoids of similar forms out of the soul energies of insects and creatures that weren't bipedal, for the purpose of putting them into labor that required hands and feet. In this way, the initial humanoids lived in a slave-like existence. This story is old but not old enough. Humanoids were created in separate segments by separate people in separate parts of the universe, since time infinity. The above story is a based upon a narrated account from a star person from Estrovakia.

Over time, the humanoid form became attractive to people who were looking to create an outwardly uniform set of people for populating a settlement. These were star people who had lost their kingdoms in wars and were left with a mix bag of few supernaturals and indigenous beings of various kinds, or had escaped persecution and had stumbled upon some humanoids of different kinds as well as some supernaturals and wanted to make them as uniform people for a new kingdom. We have humanoid form for Earth because the star administration of Earth wanted a uniform set of people who could co-exist and to not deal with individual types of intrinsic origin of people. The star people who were consigned out were almost all already in their humanoid forms of various different types from various different star nations, though some of them were in their extra-terrestrial, supernatural form. Most of the humans have mixed souls, already from what was consigned to Earth. Averagely, American souls are roughly eighty percent primate, such as ape and other monkey forms, with the rest being distributed among various other types, the most prevalent being canines, followed by felines and other primitive types.

The blueprint of the DNA (deoxyribonuleic acid) structure for the humans were decided by the star administrations of Earth, however, humanity was created and have survived in batches, accordingly some of them have slightly different genetic makeup than others. Our genetic makeup of the human DNA is also not specific to the race or the elements of air, water, earth, space and fire of places from where our ancestry upon Earth is and neither to our soul types from the stars. The brain chemistry and circuitry are defined and funneled by the Divine, so it is supposed to perform almost uniformly across the population. Over time, darker light realms have messed with the human DNA and body form to introduce pandemics and other personality disorders into the population. Additionally, the humans are created in the public heavenly system in the flavors of certain select Saurischia groups. Therefore, the human body makeup varies very slightly based upon each Saurus group's own methods of creation and element matter.

I discovered that our planet has ambulatory algorithm differentiated by the type of humanoid or soul energy of the human. It isn't same for all types of humans. The groups of humans who are marked as troublesome based upon their history of conduct upon this planet when walk upon it, they stumble clumsily. This indicates to heavenly light overseeing us that the trouble makers need to be managed down in their life.

Photo 1. Dressed as a Dark Angel for Halloween, 2015.

DARKNESS

W̶e inherently know about Darkness and worship the Devil on Halloween. I used to think of Halloween as an occasion for a Costume party. The costume that I am wearing in Photo 1. on the previous page existed before I learnt about Darkness and wrote about it in this book. The time of Halloween is actually an astronomical positioning of Earth when the crossroads between Earth and a galaxy which used to be part of the light universe but has been a part of the dark universe since a 100,000 years, opens up after the barriers become thinner. This lasts only about twenty-four hours.

Earth has a massive, hierarchical "Darkness" realm that tries to bring order and justice to humanity, but with different set of reins than the light. The light approaches with compassion and understanding waiting for the natural order of justice to take place eventually, if not in this life then the next. However, in Darkness the actions against or in favor of someone are immediate, and things are dealt with a tough hand mostly without compassion. Even innocent people get tortured severely, usually in the guise of imparted justice. Justice hasn't been happening through Darkness in the last ~100,000 years because someone got to the top of Darkness and changed the rules to suit his desires. I am asked to clarify that his initial intentions were purer, but darker things have a way of escalating like a chain reaction. Today, about 80 percent of the darkness realms are not there to bring justice or help the living but are a place of power where people let their desires loose and commit crimes, so, humanity suffers, silently, in a way not known to our cognitive selves.

Human births used to be controlled by Earth's Darkness. They used to govern allocation of parents based on their own rules, without following the real karmic laws of the divine. The children could choose their parents but not vice versa. The parents weren't allowed to choose their children. These days the human births are governed by the divine. They narrow down choice of parents based upon people's karma, evolution level, and their soul history.

Three and a half years ago, I was told by a Celtic witch that darkness is 'lack of light'. I discovered over time that it is way more than that. When people are tortured beyond the tolerance levels designed by the divine, the tortured cells that were powered by the light metamorph into a different kind of power which is of the opposite nature to that of light. In other words the energy of the tortured soul or soul-part, transforms to a state that the light doesn't permit, which is the state of lack of light and so the cells building up the soul essence and the light powers become those of darkness, so darkness energy isn't a void, or the lack of light but a real substance just not of the light anymore and it is devoid of compassion. Therefore, darkness is just a different form of power which is severed from the Light. Realms that hold and use darkness powers are called 'Darkness' realms.

In the Darkness realms, powers of darkness get harnessed into holograms and used for various kinds of purposes ranging from extremely disruptive actions of causing death or torture of people in our real physical existence to benign uses of spiritual surgery and recovery from illness.

Occasionally some of our energy is yanked out of our body and presented to Darkness for torture in lieu of something for someone and they get tortured beyond death to produce dark energies of anger, helplessness, self-pity and apathy. These parts of people become shadow-selves of themselves, working in the Darkness realms often against themselves. Darkness power is powerful enough to do some of the work that 'Divine Will' won't permit.

The divine would not supply powers to commit crime, but the darker Light realms and Darkness routinely use power to bully people, even civilizations, and brew up things up to their needs and desires. Besides using powers of Darkness, they also use previously stored powers of the light which they have harnessed mechanically. For this purpose, they usually tie up soul-parts of both the living and the dead and tether them into a program much like the players in a computer game driven by Artificial Intelligence (AI), which is an automated method of achieving something using soul energies of people. In such holograms the people are usually retarded so that they cannot think and so they could act like an automation with their Acupuncture points plugged-in to accomplish certain actions out of them. Some of such holograms or programs also use sane people who can exercise their own freewill based upon their own understandings and prejudices and so they don't really use AI in such holograms but let the souls or soul-parts decide a course of action in a flow chart with different people at different nodes. Most of these programs do not have a guided direction but are created to cause general havoc. The "evil" doers in this case call themselves haters of humanity but they aren't real political haters of humanity. Those have respect and only lead a formal war or even have mini concentration camps here and there. But the fanaticism that lead the civilizations on Earth into World Wars are driven by Darkness and smaller chunks of the Dark Universe.

CHAPTER II

TRUTH ABOUT THE KNOWN

DETERMINISM AND IN-DETERMINISM

"Random should stand for spontaneous which is also causal except for the time span of the causality event being infinitesimally small."

- Sarita Gupta

All facts and events in the Universe are deterministic, which means they exemplify natural laws of cause and effect. All things, including human choices and decisions have sufficient causes.

The classical literature states that non-deterministic algorithms may exhibit different behaviors on different runs. The available definition of a nondeterministic algorithm also states that for the same input, the algorithm can produce different outputs on different runs as opposed to a deterministic algorithm. However, this is only true because the algorithm hasn't run long enough to compare with what appears to be a deterministic algorithm. The literature also goes on to say that a non-deterministic algorithm may not finish due to the infinite size of the branching of the outputs in the form of an ever-growing tree. However, truth is that what appears as a non-deterministic algorithm, for example, a polynomial series, if run over an infinite time would converge to the same result as a deterministic algorithm would produce for the same set of inputs. If we chose to examine the output at some point before infinity, the longer it has been since the starting point on the axis of time, the closer the result will be to the output produced by the deterministic version of the algorithm.

In classical literature, a deterministic algorithm is depicted simplistically as a single line of processing through input to output, and a non-deterministic algorithm is depicted as one with branching induced by external inputs or stimuli, else the branching won't occur, arriving at different outputs for different runs ending at a given finite time, as depicted in the diagram labelled as figure 1.

Figure 1.

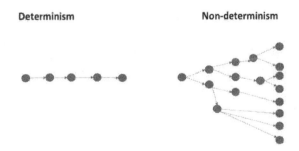

In truth, what is referred to as non-deterministic is actually deterministic and what is referred to as deterministic is a subset of the entire problem space and so it can be imagined as a part of the entire deterministic model space. This is easily demonstrated by figure 1, where I have drawn the branching and progress of the two types of algorithms on the axis of time, it is clear that if we redefine non-determinism as determinism then determinism is just a subset of non-determinism whereby it is just one of the paths on the tree for what is labelled as non-determinism. Therefore, the distinction between the nomenclatures of determinism and non-determinism should not exist and all things in the Universe is deterministic because the universe runs on causality and Causal Determinism states that for every effect there is a definite cause, likewise for each cause there is a definite effect.

I believe that for certain applications people wanted to simplify the universal problem space of causality into a snapshot of the result or the output, and trace back from that node representing the output, to the root cause. This provided them with a linear equation from input to output which people started calling a deterministic equation or algorithm. Additionally, people did not want to evaluate the trajectory of a phenomenon from beginning to end over that infinite axis of time and so they would take a much smaller segment on the time axis and that part of the algorithm would not look like it would have much possibility of branching out because the possibilities of external stimuli causing the branching would be minimal and so approximation to a linear algorithm wasn't a bad idea. Once this linear subset of the entire problem space came to be known as determinism, real determinism or the universal set of the problem space came to be known as indeterminism almost as a synonym for non-fathomable because it is hard to chase down all the possibilities and the subsequent branching especially in the case of algorithms that would run in polynomial time, and in some scenarios where the problem space is fairly linear wait long enough on the time scale to detect a possible branching. Therefore, Computer Science is a working approximation of Metaphysics.

CONVERGENCE AND DIVERGENCE THEORY

"Life is a Stochastic Process."
- Sarita Gupta

In the big picture, the Convergence Theory portrays the catch-up effect for situations. It can be applied to any situation where there is a need for overall balance to kick in for things to stay sustained for a prolonged period of time.

If a sequence of random numbers converges to some limit, then it is convergent, else it is divergent. The balance between both convergent and divergent processes is the natural order of the Cosmos. Almost all that we do, and experience can be summarized as a balanced mix of convergent and divergent actions and reactions.

A Divergence Series doesn't keep diverging forever and it seems that way only because at some point the leaf nodes that kind of disappears get converted into other forms of energy or jump onto other processes that could very well be convergent in nature. An example would be an explosion of an atom bomb that kicks of a fission reaction which is supposed to go on forever with the molecules of the radioactive fuel branching out but at some point those molecules get transformed into other kinds of energy thereafter entering a different kind of a process or action or mutation. For example, when they get pierced into the bodies of people in the surroundings they react with other molecules in the body and the resulting substance is different. People suffer from radioactive decay for prolonged periods of time only if a fair amount of it stays concentrated in one region without mutating over time with other molecules. Some of the molecules also mutate with the soil after which the fission reaction does not continue. Thus, a divergent process does not remain divergent over infinite time however if we take a snapshot before the leaf nodes have taken onto another form it looks like it is going to diverge forever.

A lot of dust from our life problems settle over time just like a Convergence Series converges to a smaller limit onto stability over time. A rudimentary explanation of how Convergence Theory works in receiving justice is that when one injustice does not receive justice fully within a reasonable time, it generates other transgressions like a ripple effect which infuriates other people into creating misdeeds upon others and when our enemies' enemies have been attacked, we may find some friends or neutral people to help us out. So, what goes around comes around.

Figure 1. is a sketch of a Cauchy sequence which is a convergent series where the highs and the lows minimize over time onto a more stable state.

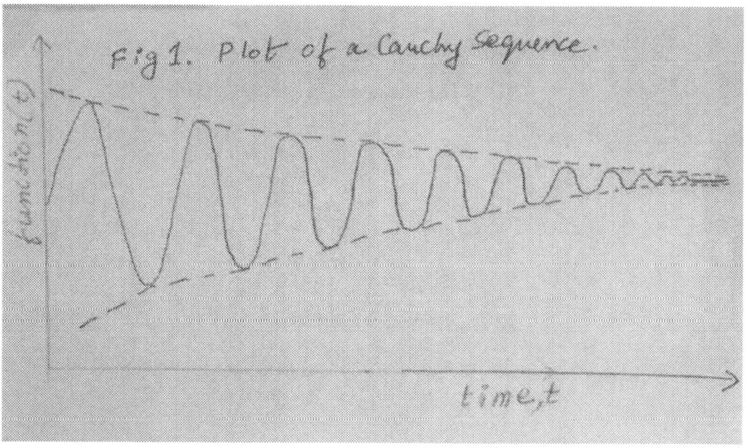

Fig 1. Plot of a Cauchy sequence.

The natural motions of the Universe can be explained with the analogy of water in a pond as representative of the balanced collective karma of people within a subset of the Universe. When we throw a stone in the pond, the dip in the water level does get fixed eventually as the impact arising out of that dip travels outwards on a Divergence Series to the available mass of water in all directions where eventually the surrounding water body absorbs that impact and the dip is leveled out. This is analogous to the people who suffered in the dip due to the external attack of the stone hitting them, receiving relief with their problems being gradually absorbed by the surrounding people.

Taking a more in-depth look at what happens after the stone hits the pond, a research paper by Emmanuel Fort of the Langevin Institute in Paris, France, and his colleagues, states that the equations governing the behavior of waves not only have ripples fanning out in concentric circles from the point of the dropped stone but at some point when the ripples have reached the outside rim of the pond they reflect back to the center like a reversed movie of the dropped stone but we never actually see this happening because it has only an infinitesimally small chance that an outside circle would form spontaneously in the water. Just for the purpose of understanding, let's say we have a round tub of water with its level still. If we subtly drop this tub down, then there will be a jolt to the outside rim which would create concentric circles converging in from the outside to the center. The paper by Fort says that the backward-travelling waves converge exactly on their starting point, just as if you were rewinding time. The reversed waves converge to recreate their original shape though the size of the retreating waves is much smaller because the momentum is reduced because most of the energy is already spent upon resistance from adjoining water particles while the waves were fanning out. The paper says that the waves continue to travel out again once they have converged at the central point, and this continues back and forth over infinite time.

For practical purposes, we would palpably observe only about a to and a fro from the center to the rim of the pond, and a second much smaller to and a fro of the movement of the waves of water. This is also true of other kinds of waves such as light and sound if they experience similar external input analogous to a stone hitting the pond.

An exception to the laws of Divergence and Convergence is achieved by Time Machines. Time can really mess with the natural flow of the Cosmic laws. For example, in the case of the stone hitting a pond, the waves won't fan out from the center. Fort's paper corroborates, "A real time-reversal would have a sink that absorbs all the waves."

To escape concoctions of Time Machines which routinely interfere with the flow of the Universe, one of the light realms had created a realms had created a zone free of time for energetic or spiritual work such as healing to happen without the interference of time slices that aren't natural, but reversed, halted, put back in the past, put into the future, put in a rut or a cycle, warped and so on. This zone is known as Infinity. It is represented by the sign for infinity shown in Figure 2.

Figure 2.

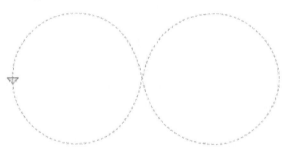

The symbol for Infinity in Figure 2 can be explained mathematically as that the concept of Infinity has two ends, positive and negative with each side across the point of zero, mapping infinitely to the circular track generating and destroying natural as well as affected systems in the universe, to together encompass all possibilities, choices, and occurrence.

Process Model diagram 1.

a.m. ---> i.m.

\+

d.m. ---> d.m.

\+

i.m.

In the Abstract mathematical model of infinity as infinite we may break it down in the form of adjacent representation, where abstract model is abbreviated as a.m., infinite model is abbreviated as i.m. and discrete model is abbreviated as d.m.

Figure 3 below, shows the derivation steps of the complete, mathematical model of infinity, leading to the initial Figure 2.

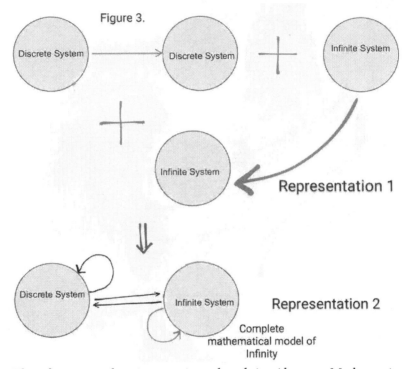

Figure 3.

Therefore new theories are introduced in Abstract Mathematics, stating:

i.   The spontaneity of occurrence of Discrete processes are needed to complete the theoretical abstract picture of infinity to be infinite.

ii. A Discrete system within itself also employs the infinitely possible Abstract Mathematics algorithms to exiexist

iii. If the Discrete model remains discrete forever then Infinity is not infinite.

iv. A Discrete system may latch on to an Infinite system at the end of its life cycle to continue on.

FREEWILL

The good news says that we have freewill, when we don't. For context the holy scriptures used to be sometimes referred as the good news in archaic theosophical literature. On the topic of freewill, determinism says that all events including moral choices are completely determined by previously existing events.

We would like to think that we have freewill. Religion teaches us that we have freewill. They aren't wrong. Adhering to the classical definition of determinism, religion is deterministic. Most religion have their set of spiritual laws or holy scriptures which is only a subset of that entire hologram of light, and hence it doesn't include the entire Collective Consciousness, nor the causal space that includes all possibilities of choices, nor the possibility of changes in behavior to the trajectory of output to whatever we willed, due to the varying partial derivatives of the will of other's consciousnesses over time. In layman terms, our religion doesn't include what happens to us by people of other religion or how we should treat them or what happens to us by star people or what we do to them and even the dos and don'ts of virtue are rather simplistic and doesn't include the entire gamut of the deviant mind. Our minds are connected to the entire Universe. The religious leaders who laid down the rules and wrote the spiritual laws attempted well on working with a subset of the approximation of the Universe and people follow their morals in their daily lives and lead a collectively ok life, but we do see cases where we say, "God, we didn't deserve this", "the wretched", "the underdogs", "the godforsaken". These are the people who have seen the bad side of the Time Gods and so are warped into misery and hence would not receive justice because the natural divergence of their problem away from them mitigating and assuaging their issues were blocked due to negative time tactics, the Universe is big and the balance of convergence and divergence still works but takes much longer. That is why we say, "Time heals all."

What happens to us is truth, the scriptures are laws, they aren't truth. The laws serve us as a good motto to follow in life but doesn't solve our problems once we have found ourselves in a hole. It is like being in the dip where a stone hits a pond and after some ripples fanning out on the Divergence Series and then converging back into the initial dip on a Convergence Series, the hole looks covered.

To demonstrate that we actually do not have freewill, let's look at the graph in Figure 1, below. I want to first clarify that by determinism we mean classical or canonical indeterminism of which classical determinism is a subset, as I have already explained in the chapter which is titled as "Determinism and Indeterminism". Within the restricted problem space where we exclude the probable, outsider influences, where we consider only the person represented by the Blue dots, it looks like we have freewill to decide whatever for the choices from the beginning to the end of the life path, thereby revealing possible outcomes based upon our own choices, but usually

Figure 1.

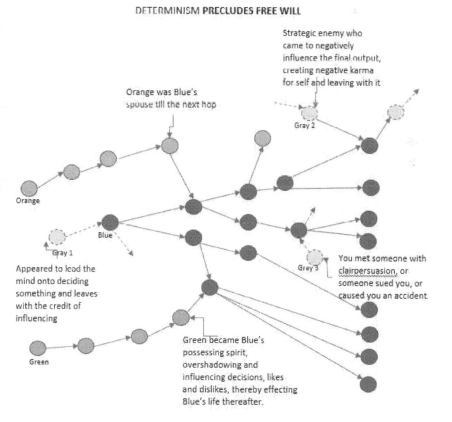

DETERMINISM **PRECLUDES FREE WILL**

Strategic enemy who came to negatively influence the final output, creating negative karma for self and leaving with it

Orange was Blue's spouse till the next hop

Gray 2

Orange

Blue

Gray 1

Appeared to lead the mind onto deciding something and leaves with the credit of influencing

Gray 3

You met someone with clairpersuasion, or someone sued you, or caused you an accident.

Green became Blue's possessing spirit, overshadowing and influencing decisions, likes and dislikes, thereby effecting Blue's life thereafter.

Green

in the real world the likes of the orange, green and gray exist who continually reduce our freewill. They could be your spouses, friends, enemies, possessing spirits and other entities sketched out in the scenarios in figure 1. The more we consider the entire Collective Consciousness and the entire Universe all of which do influence each bit of our will in however infinitesimally small amounts, we end up with no freewill.

Given we have no free will, how would good things ever happen to us? This is where Karma kicks in. We should receive justice for ourselves within the rights of our own individual karma, as guaranteed by the divine model of life. Keeping our Karma up is important, and the Convergence Theory ensures us all that we will receive justice but for some of us it can take a long time especially if we have chosen to be a martyr. Light teaches us to shine our light as bright as we can and not let anyone dull our sparkle. Keeping hope is also good. It sends out a signal to the light which includes our own gods or whatever we worship and also benign light that is above and beyond them as well, saying that we are expectant of receiving justice and relevant good things coming our way.

Could we have free will ever at all? Ideally everyone is entitled to run their own mind's and follow their own hearts and exhibit their own personalities. This is almost possible if everyone tries to live and let live and try to be just and righteous. But, sometimes big mistakes happen the effects of which reverberates for too long and it looks like people haven't received justice for eons and the light starts feeling cold and people start to lose faith and resort to darkness, but soon they realize that darkness and light are the biggest dichotomy of energy in the entire Universe and it is not a long-term place for people who sprang from the light. The only way one can do one's job of enforcing one's will or volition for their cause is to be relentlessly active in the readjustment or even repurposing of one's will in the event of a hindrance or obstacle thrown in by classical indeterminism into realizing their purpose to make their will stand, or in the worst case try to at least receive justice in some other form of remuneration for one's efforts.

For us to have freewill a lot of the Universe has to start anew. Where we are right now would look like a chart of a stochastic process representing the justice-injustice imbalance among random people. The imbalances in the give-and-take are rather high, not among just individuals but among races of people, sections of society, nations, whole star nations and even sections of the universe. Some of the imbalances are between rulers and subjects of monarchical places, between progeny and ancestors and between the teachers and pupils especially the spiritual teachers. Some of this randomness were necessary to bring justice to the biggest victim so that the collective Karma could even out.

Photo 1. taken in the woods of Western Washington.

COLLECTIVE CONSCIOUSNESS

All scientific explanation of the Collective Consciousness is that people's energy bodies or Chakras are connected to other people's Chakras by threads known as energetic cords. These connections are not just between people but also between a person and an artifact such as a thought, a time-slice, a hologram or a realm. We often talk about them as the following examples.

"Cords of attachment."

"Striking a connection."

"Dependent personality disorder."

"Holding onto a thought."

"Clinging onto the past."

"Entwined with someone."

"Soulmate connection."

"Karmic connection."

"Social ties."

We are emotionally or mentally connected to certain people in our lives because we are spiritually connected. This connection literally looks like threads or ropes of energy depending upon how strong the connection is.

In shamanic lore and even in Norse mythology the Collective Consciousness is analogues to the World Tree or the Yggdrassil. In some cultures, it is also known as the Tree of Life. The Photo 1. on page 92, almost looks like a Tree of Life, with proliferate branches reaching upwards to the light and roots multiplying into the depths of the soil. In shamanic culture the light is known as the "Upper World" and the etheric realm of Earth which is considered to be beneath the soil is called the "Lower World". In cognitive Psychology, the Upper World is the superconsiousness supporting life and helping our brains function and the Lower World represents the subconsciousness. Both, the part of us connected to the superconsious and the parts of us delving deep within us in our subconscious affect us in our waking consciousness along with the external stimuli and our reactions to them. In the middle of writing the last sentence I had paused to confirm, "Do we act on our own?" I saw a dark light lord who seemed to consider himself a master Physicist, wake up from a sleeping bench and reply, "Not really." In sleep, the external stimuli is absent except for flies, ghosts, star people, non-dreams and dreams. A proof-reader asked, "How many people you think would get the humor in the last sentence?" I didn't have an answer. I sat there for about five minutes and still couldn't come up with an answer.

For more context, throughout my writing process, I had access to some of the invisible people in some of the invisible realms of Earth as well as the stars and in the light as well. Hence, I could receive a reply after posing a question.

Collective Consciousness really mean that more often than not the individual consciousnesses are not separate like we think. The souls in the universe are like molecules of water in an ocean where they intermingle automatically most with those in their vicinity and then least with the ones that they have not met or are far away. The waves, the tides and even the wake of a ship which are all external factors cause some forced intermingling among the water molecules which wouldn't mingle otherwise just like how unforeseen circumstances bring people together. However, a bigger tsunami causes more mingling just like a war or a mass movement of political refugees would cause, and when there is a really big tectonic shift all of the water mass of the ocean is affected collectively just like what some of the star-wars would do to us. However, the people in the Universe are not always as segregated as the water bodies are but are more connected to each other indirectly via the uber divine hologram which isn't always true due to energy barriers created between star nations to block off outside energy, though these energy barriers usually get broken and recreated or restructured during wars.

I once came across a book that taught to surrender to fate. It talked about going with the flow, which is a good thing, however one must pay their bills and always try to be ethical. Surrendering to life is a good thing. Being passive is not bad, it just means one has faith, fate will catch up, if not one's own then the collective fate of people which are tied together through the Collective Consciousness.

I was going through a questionnaire that asked how I may have changed through the process of writing this book. The insights into real life situations that I gained while writing this book is that the divine doesn't care about single people but the collective souls or the Collective Consciousness of people. If someone is willing to sacrifice for the good of another, the divine doesn't say no, no matter how much they give away all they ever had. This does create an anomaly the balanced collective karma of the Collective Consciousness because someone was left behind and hadn't received their justice as compared to other people in their lives and their surroundings. To these people all that I can say is to have faith. Good things eventually happen to good people. One of the basic tenets of the Universe is justice for all.

Given we are talking about nature bringing us justice, a proof-reader wanted to know about the limits of crime nature would allow.

Each individual soul has their own allocated powers for their sustenance of life and carrying their will through their lives, but a soul's powers aren't enough to cause a catastrophe at a scale larger than what the divinely set limits of perpetration of havoc would allow. Hence the darker Light realms, harness and utilize light energy of individuals to make a powerful hologram to enslave these souls into carrying out almost anything that the limits of the Collective Karma would allow for the purposes of perpetration of havoc.

Another insight I gained in the process of writing this book is that vengeance is not a sin. It is an act of bringing justice, to self and to others, and collectively to the Collective Consciousness. Darkness has strict rules of vengeance and I learnt to appreciate it. Then I paused and wanted to interview the divine about its take on vengeance. The divine channeled the following to me:

"In the eyes of the divine, vengeance is not seen as vengeance. It is seen as an act of bringing attention of the 'sinner' to the havoc they are causing upon others and how it felt for them. This process opens their mind to the existence of such suffering, thus gaining wisdom. Through wisdom we learn to empathize. As a balancing act, growing empathy grows the left side of our brain which is the seat of mathematical intelligence. This in turn, grows one up to be able to funnel higher powers of the divine due to being closer to that infinite intelligence."

SACRED SYMBOLS FUNNELING LIFE

The sacred symbols are not just a painting or a religious artifact, but they are a way of connecting to the real hologram of that symbol. Most people who appreciate or pray looking at one of these symbols do not connect to the real hologram and do not get their prayers answered. I am told that only about 20 percent of the people actually connect to the specific matrix of the energy supporting the sacred symbol and had their prayers answered. These energy matrices are like an input-out based computer program and some funnel powers of a certain hologram belonging to a Lightish realm, and some of these holograms are made up of other energies with their own separate consciousness who indirectly channel various kinds of powers from above supporting life and regeneration, maintaining brain functioning, and trying to bring justice to people.

I have tried to make sense of the Egyptian magic and their death rituals in the last five years, but the information available to us did not agree with my innate senses. The literature on this subject evoke mystery but don't reveal much. I learnt that the Egyptian magic is proprietary because it is from Obalesk, Arborra, Cetus, and Sirius and almost all of it originated in Arborra and Obalesk. Among the star nations that have bigger stars, the powers are higher, and most of the warfare employs legerdemain, so they need to protect their powers and magic, and hence due to the proprietary nature of the subject the Hieroglyphics do not reveal much.

The available books on Egyptian History talk about the Sun God "Ra" or "Re". Ra isn't a person's name. It is pronounced as Reh, in the language of Obalesk, a star in the Aboh constellation. Reh is the vermilion disc which is worn as a coronet by people from Aboh, after their canonization which enables them to funnel higher powers from the relics and the Elemental spirits there. In the photos of "Ra" in the media, the depicted bird-people are a species, known as Abeeht which originated in Obalesk since that star existed. The Obalesk star has existed since 1 trillion years ago and has been rebuilt a few times since then. Abeehts are powerful birds and the ones that had attained 'Shaman'-hood, Shaman being an Obalesk word for high priest, have helped the Pharaohs on Earth in their work towards saving Earth and nurturing humanity. However, they aren't from the Sun of Earth. They are from Obalesk which is about 128 lightyears away from the Earth. In Obalesk, the top echelon Abeeht who is canonized, is worshipped as their Sun God. The translations of the Hieroglyphic are lost in time. These days the video games suggest that Ra is the name of a God but that isn't true. Ra is the vermillion disk from Aboh which is pronounced as "Reh" in their language. The Photo 1. depicts a canonized level-one Abeeht from the Obalesk star.

Photo 1. by Sarita Gupta, the Sun God "Ra" at the Abu Simbel temple.

I found out that almost all of the magic on Earth are derived from Arborra, Aboh, Cetus, and Sirius' relics and magic constructs based off of their elements of Alchemy and the Elemental powers. The Egyptian Hieroglyphics talk about the Hathor people. They are a humanoid race from Arborra and some of the other neighboring stars and planets they had settled or rebuilt. The Cetus galaxy which is much farther and in a different supercluster has been under the rule of the Hathors since the last 4 million years, so a lot of their magic is derived from the Hathor magic.

The Korean Kabich which is a version of the Ankh which is also called the "Key of life" is originally from the Hathor galaxy. It was integrated in the Korean royalty by the Hathor royalty when one of them had incarnated on Earth as a star-seed and was the king of Korea.

The Freemasonic Eye used to be powered by the Darkness realms of Earth and it is derived from the Wadjet which made its way from the Hathor civilization to the Cetus galaxy where it is known as the Uwajj. I am not writing details here because of the proprietary nature of the knowledge.

The Illuminati's magic symbols are also powered by the Uwajj which is also known as "The eye of Ra". It is not the "Sun God Ra"'s own eye. The Uwajj is like a Tablet of darkness magic used in conjunction with other forms of power sources.

Solomon's Temple magic was also powered by the Hathors. His high priest used to be an earthly incarnate of a past Hathor king's father.

The Kabbalistic Tree of Life is powered by the darkness, al-chemical and elemental powers of the original Jewish people, thirty percent of who were commissioned out to Earth to be a human. The Jewish sub-race of the Hathors came to Arborra about 900 billion years ago as conquerors after Arborra existed, but within a 100,000 years they became the prisoners of war of Arborra, so they are now a minority race of Arborra. As I thought I was done writing this, the soul-part of someone famous stopped by and said, "Didn't I offer you marriage, and I am a Jew." I looked at him and remembered that he is Jewish on Earth but not by his origin in the stars. For further information he does comedies and the sense of humor shows. I then realized that I needed to clarify here that among today's Jewish population only about forty-seven percent have a fair amount of their soul energy from their origin in the stars, rest have different varying origins in the stars.

You may have noticed that many emblems and some of the secret societies have the wings somewhere in their logo. About thirty percent of the wing symbols on Earth trace their roots back to the protectively open winged hologram of the Arborra star, however in the last few hundred thousand years about 20 percent of the wings are from the Cetus galaxy and 10 percent from Obalesk and rest from other parts of the Hathor galaxy. The wings of Arborra are depicted in the Photo 2. where it adorns the doorway.

Photo 2. by Sarita Gupta, depicting the sacred symbols of the
Abu Simbel temple built by Ramesses II.

The Islamic Black Stone in Mecca is powered by a relic from Sirius. The relic inside the Black stone, was sent to Earth in ~7250 B.C. About 3500 years ago, the pre-islamic people of the region put this relic inside the Black stone in Mecca.

The Trishul or the Trident is very ancient and made its way from the stars. Some of the Indian deities, such as Durga and Shiva carry the Trident. The Trishul is a powerful "Yantr" or a mythical tool used in defending oneself against enemies, not just physically but also spiritually. A version of the Trident also exist in the Mongol culture.

The Om symbol on the flag in Photo 3 below is found widely in the temples of northern India. Another symbol that is as widely found in India is the Swastik symbol.

Photo 3. at Bhairo Temple, Mount Kailash, India

After my clairvoyance opened the first sacred symbol that appeared to help me out of certain situations was the one shown in the photo below. It is the three-disc holy protective matrices that the deities are holding which act like a cobweb for catching curses and negatively intrusive energies. Each of the discs were woven by light of different colors and wavelengths to cure affliction caused by evil.

Photo 4, taken during Durga Puja at Kolkata, India.

Growing up, the hologram that I have worshipped most is the Eye followed by the Ankh which are a proprietary hologram meant only for the people of the Hathor galaxy who have had lives of those origins for more than a million lives. The Ankh supports regeneration of life and powers of protection from enemies and negativity and helps keep people full of life with their soul energy active and inside the body and helps in the event of attack or imminent death by some means. It also helps in keeping disease away.

Photo by Sarita Gupta, taken in June 2019.

The Epsilon is a Sacred Geometry used by many divinely supported work such as the functioning of the human brain. The epsilon has been worshipped widely by many. The Greek version of it represented by $E\psi\iota\lambda o\nu$ has been widely used by some of their early Mathematicians, Philosophers and Metaphysicists. The epsilon is manipulated to produce the Nuclear Fusion reaction and widely used in supporting functions of life and even helps in growing the fertilized zygote into a baby.

WHEEL OF LIFE

C ycle of life or the "Wheel of Life" is most studied by the Buddhists. The Hathors have created most of humanity but have cradled the Siberians, the Egyptians, and the Nepalese, mainly because they lived there on and off, in the last million years. There is also more power near the Himalayas and the Buddhists being from northern India and Nepal which is at the foothills of the Himalayas, in general have higher spiritual skills and can see dead people so they have spent more time and effort in understanding death and the cycle of life. The Buddhist wheel of life is just a depiction of morals and actions needed to ascend from Earth and go to a realm of light without future births upon Earth or get incorporated back into the star nations from which these humans were consigned out, after appropriate review and paper work and redemption from relevant people and authorities. Buddhists and Lamas sit by the image of the Wheel of Life and meditate. It is a good way to connect to the divine since by looking at it we express the desire to evolve out of our shortcomings and embrace higher thoughts and compassion to greater emotional intelligence.

After my "clairs" opened up, I found that dead people have souls and souls do not perish. They just wander around in various locations waiting to be born again as a child. This cycle of existence seems meaningless. Seems life should have never existed.

I wrote the above paragraph a year ago, on my own. Then I spoke to the light about "life" and received the following knowledge transmission.

About 1.3 trillion years ago, there was an enormous mass of moving matter through space with no light in it. It was like a Thoughtform. It stole a huge amount of light into it. Thus, a star was created. That star chunked lives out of itself. Those lives consisted of the elements of the matter of the star and light. They were chunked out in hierarchies of king, queen, children and other people in a strict hierarchy for living and sustenance of a whole civilization with different work for different hierarchy of people to support all in a society.

Today, light thinks that should not have happened. The stars and planets formed out of nebulae of generated matter and stolen light spun out of control and life in various forms also spun out of control. The population of Earth alone including dead humans is 9.2 billion.

I was writing the section under, "What light would like today" and someone channeled some falsehood which sounded catastrophic, at which point, a real light being that I had never met before, came and asked me to erase and rectify into the following:

"Total surrender from the stars of their makings such as people and planets, to the light.

Then people will get justice for each, according to their deeds since that 1.6 trillion years ago.

Do not be scared. Light won't be separated from matter. It is too late for that.

However slowly we would be returning some light that was not part of the scheme of life, a billion years ago."

All sentient beings from Earth have had past incarnations. We stop incarnating on Earth after ascension to the 5th dimension or higher in terms of our wisdom, compassion, cleared chakras and kundalini awakening which is a terminology from Eastern understanding of ascension. Other nomenclature for ascension are Moksha and Nirvana.

There is a terminology called oversoul which includes energy of a soul from current incarnation if alive and summation of all of the past lives. After death, an individual's soul goes to the light and becomes one with the oversoul energy. However, some people do not want to go to the light and go to a "Lightish" place which is like a realm of the dead where they retain identity of individual souls and stay separate or as a mix of a certain number of lives until their next birth when they incarnate in one piece or as a mix of pieces of their oversoul energy. Using the Euler diagram analogy, the oversoul is the Universal Set, U with each incarnation as a set within this Universal set. This is depicted in Figure 1. below. The different lives or sets may intersect or not and they usually overlap partially and sometimes may overlap fully. An incarnation of an individual consists of any mix of energy from their oversoul whether it came from the light or Lightish in certain percentages of certain past lives which aren't necessarily chronological. Usually the entire soul energy doesn't make to the Light or the Lightish and remain lost in the "Middle World" or stay in captivity with nature spirits such as trees, mountains, rivers and oceans. These soul parts almost never make to the Light or to birth on to the next incarnation unless a spiritual healer retrieves them and sends them to the light for the next or later birth. Figure 1. shows a rudimentary example of the concept of an oversoul via a Venn diagram.

I found the following reasons why people reincarnate:

❖ Reincarnation is just a chain-like process like how a tree grows up and bear fruits, sheds seeds and then germinate and grow up again to repeat a cycle.

❖ Reincarnation is a karmic process of regeneration of atoms and molecules of the soul energy.

Then I wondered why some people have lives back-to-back and why some people have not had an incarnation for millions and even billions of years. Some of these people stay in the light universe somewhere and some get sent to the dark universe.

Figure 1.

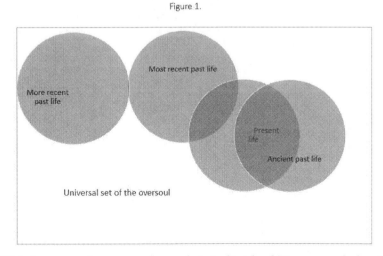

This happens because of people's individual Karma and also the collective Karma of the Collective Consciousness. Sometimes people need to be put on the back burner where they are usually vaulted by enemies and even by well-wishers or are put into oblivion in Darkness. This happens due to unknown needs of the Universe.

By the doctrine of the Wheel of Life, reincarnation is targeted towards evolving people off of their past mistakes, patterns and karma.

Reincarnation is not limited to ancestries of a particular race which vary across incarnations and not typified by the origins of our souls. Our souls are typically what was commissioned out of the stars and is from one or more places of extra-terrestrial origin and remains that way no matter where and to whom we were born across different incarnations as a human. In my past-life regression healing sessions, I have had varied reactions from people who discovered that in some of their past lives they were of a race different than their own.

In one of my past life regression sessions with a famous musician, I had introduced him to his past-life soul parts for spiritual healing. The soul parts were of different race than his own. One was Italian and the other one was White American from the 1800s. From their demeanor, height and even looks, It was easy to guess that they could be parts of an oversoul, born in different human ancestry, for their bodies. They resembled each other in body language. He stared at them for a long minute and then went quiet. I wanted to know if my client believed me about the fact that they were his past lives. He said, "I believe that they are my past lives, but I can't wrap my head around all those years of discrimination I felt in my heart for being Black." He then exchanged greetings with his past-life soul-parts. They mostly stared at each other with a longing full of emotions we display when we meet someone dear after a long time; it was also like how we see someone after a long time, unexpectedly, and want to know if it is real. They didn't share much words. Much later one of the soul-parts told me that he was thankful to have had the opportunity to exchange a greeting, face-to-face with his forward life.

Some proof-readers wanted to know how I showed his dead past life soul-parts to the musician. There are too many spiritual ways to achieve that. One can time-travel and go back to the past and actually meet them real-time though still in the past, or one can create a time-window out of which one can view the past like watching a prerecorded movie. It is also possible to call forth the dead soul-parts, like I have explained in the "bringing a realm to one's location" in the chapter, "The Invisible realms of Earth." Here we call forth the past life souls or soul-parts and interact with them real-time but from across a barrier window like in videoconferencing. They would look like standing behind an invisible TV screen even though they would look like they are in the same room being able to see and talk to the living. When we go near them and try to touch or hold them, their physical consistency would feel like smoke or thin air and we won't be able to really touch them however we would perceive them as a gust of wind of normal air over us, or cold air if they are from Darkness. From across the window of "videocon-ferencing", where the remote party experiences us as remote across their own monitor screen, the dead in the room also perceive the living to be like thin air or smoke. From the point of view of Physics, coming in close contact or colliding with the dead would feel like two blobs of energy coming in contact or colliding with each other. It is not one solid person such as us and one apparition of smoke such as the ghost colliding. Both parties would have similar consistency in the window of interaction which occurs due to thinned barriers between those two realms through which energy of the living and the dead are perceivable due to infiltration of their realm onto our human realm. Without infiltration the dead or even the soul-parts of the living would be imperceivable.

Five months later, I asked the musician about if he had some words to share for this book. He said, "It took time to bring myself to talk to them. Few weeks after, it was like before. Nothing changed. My people were still discriminated. Same slurs. Though, I view life differently now. I think of us as victims for no reason. I don't participate in the topic of race, feels less important."

Photo by Sarita Gupta, the Abu Simbel temple built by Ramessess II, also known as Ramessess the Great.

DEATH AND THE AFTERLIFE

Almost every time when we resort to self-help books there is a case of being under the influence of dead people. Even though it may sound scary, the ghosts do exist, possessions do occur, and there are always wounds and soul-parts who interact with the middle word and other ghosts and soul-parts of other people. It is just that the cognitive self in our three-dimensional reality is not aware of it.

When we get possessed by the dead or other forms of spirits, nothing really changes dramatically like the horror movies show. Who you are changes. If you represent yourself as a color Red and someone represented by a color Green possesses then you become a bit of an Orange but your credit cards remain same, your passport remains same, your body remains same and so you still live, life moves on.

Death is something everyone fears. I also used to consider death as a final annihilation of one's existence. When we die, our elements die first, and then the soul goes out, after which the elements wither gradually, leaving behind skeletal remains. Then our souls usually take up residence in a living human body. If we are lucky, then we go to the Light of the real divine. Many times, we go to a Lightish realm or to a Darkness realm depending upon our connections, present and past. So, at the time of dying, people don't lose anything other than the body and the material belongings.

The dead people living in the bodies of progeny or other people influence the minds of the living, effecting their decisions and choices in life. In such situations, the host never gets to fully express their own desires into being, so they don't really live their own life. That is why there are Phraseology like the following that exist among us. Underneath the covers they actually pertain to Possession Illness:

"She or he is a host of problems."

"Are you out of your minds?"

"He is beside himself."

"She is so like her mother!"

"The walls have ears."

I spoke to several dead celebrities who had died recently. I wanted to know how they feel about it. One of them who was famous worldwide, said that he learnt from rumors that he was murdered by star people and goons in Darkness. These "goons" are dead humans that are in control of certain powers in a certain hierarchy. Like all other ghosts, the celebrity can see, hear and talk to other ghosts but living people do not see him nor hear him. He said that sometimes he would go visit his children and watch them. Occasionally he would feel the urge of intervening something or offering them advice about something, but they couldn't see him nor hear him speak. He was aware that they wouldn't be able to interact with him but his desire to be heard and be part of people who were family was still profound. He does live and can feel and interact with people but just on a different plane or coordinates of existence which would be considered a non-physical reality for the living. Sometimes ghosts etched him in poor bodies for their own entertainment. They liked watching very rich people living meagerly and agonizing over not being able to use their own money from when they were alive.

When I started doing Energy Healing for people a year ago, I researched more on doing psychopomp work. I was thereafter introduced to the Pearly Gates by a light-being. There was a gatekeeper and a gate and supposedly dead people behind that gate. I met the "Gate Keeper" and he seemed divine. I had held the intention of going to the Four Directions. I remember going to four such gates, each with a different gate keeper. I did not delve deeper to find out which gates these were. I was told only the dead can cross those gates. Then I learnt techniques to do de-possession work popularly known among the healers as "depo" work whereby possessing beings are sent to the Light or wherever else they deserve to go so that they don't come back to haunt the living.

People may have heard about exorcism. I used to hold the opinion that exorcism was a dark and violent process which put people in danger of being possessed by more spirits than get any better. I had learnt about compassionate methods of de-possession from a Hawaiian shaman, which seemed more effective. I had heard stories of exorcism from her which sounded as scary as what the media have featured, therefore I stayed away from that subject. After further paranormal experience with possessing spirits in the months following my visit to the Shaman, I thought that I might as well draw the differences between the two different schools of de-possession work. So, I pondered. Then I saw the ghost of a Pope appear and say, "The difference between exorcism and de-possession is that in exorcism the possessing spirits are asked to leave, while in the current de-possession work, the possessing spirits are sent to another part of the body and quietened." That was something new I learnt. I had actually attended Pope John Paul II's sermon in December 2007, at the St. Peter's Basilica in the Vatican City.

St. Peter's Basilica, the Vatican City in 2007.

It seems that the style of de-possession work that some of the Energy healers do mostly sends the possessing spirits to a sandboxed realm from one part of the body to another, which makes it feel like the ghost is gone but really boxed up and so it cannot influence the host or get out of the body and do anything but lay dormant within the body itself but still festering as an inanimate foreign energy causing disease.

After I finished writing the above paragraph, a soul-part of an energy healer who I know stopped by to say that all the spirits that she had removed had left the body. In my energy healing sessions too, the spirits had actually left the body and went elsewhere through relevant portals to different realms underneath the uppermost layers of Earth or to realms outside the Earth. So, without exorcism only about half of the time the possessing spirits leave the body. Then I heard someone from among my invisible audience mutter:

"Well then going to a priest would be a good idea."

"Going to priest would not work," someone else commented.

I wondered why. Then the spirit of a high clergy stopped by to clarify:

"The priests are ordinary. There are many of them. They are devout, but they are not the chosen handful in the world who can do real de-possession work. Most of the people do not have heavy duty ghosts in their bodies. The ones who do, need a higher attention which only about five to ten people can accomplish."

A spirit who helps in psychopomp work and other Light work whom I had polled about if he wanted to send out a message through this chapter, channeled the following:

I know the present Pope. I wanted to do 'Light' work on Earth. I wanted to teach the sermons of my ancestors and their ancestors. But I learnt too much truth about the fake light-workers who interfere with work. They are really a different kind of thugs who steal benevolent people's innocence. They mislead them into darkness.

I worked hard on trying to get the dead safely across the Light and tried to make sure that the realm across the Light where the dead spends time upon themselves and wait for their next incarnation is a place in the real light and governed by real divine beings. I have succeeded in doing Light work many times and have even spoken to some "Gatekeepers" including the ones who were at the threshold of the realm of dead people in the shamanic Directions. On one occasion, after two days some dead people were brought out of the Light using forces of darkness and Alchemy. They were then tortured after being brought back. This happened only to the dead rich people and royalty. I suppose in spiritual reality it is hard to win against the number game where we aren't protected by the laws of the land and our bodyguards.

CONTENTS OF THE UNIVERSE

The Universe always existed in varying chunks and sizes of consciousnesses or souls. Here, a consciousness means an entity who can observe, think, feel, choose, has will and can act. It could be as small as an ant or as big as the spirit of a star. The Universe does not have a linear time axis of existence. It always existed in space in some form or the other. The space of the entire universe, of the light universe and the dark universe has not changed.

The universe is mostly made up of the following:

- ❖ Pure Dark Energy, which makes a big part of the Universe. The way light is a power and a source, in the same way darkness is a power and a source.
- ❖ Dark Matter, which forms the elements of the planets and people, other forms of life, and artifacts of the parts of the universe powered by the Pure Dark Energy. The people who

originate from these planets do best with the dark energy versus the light energy. The planets in the dark universe have no day light but have about one shade of rays or atmosphere which feels like dusk or dawn most of the time and some are even pitch dark. These planets have not been charted on Earth's astronomical maps and only about a hundred humans knew about them consciously. The people from these parts of the Universe are usually benign to star people. Justice happens better in their world, where usually good people do good, and bad people don't prevail for long.

❖ Light Matter, which makes up the stars which emit light, planets, and star people, all matters of Earth and us.

❖ Pure Light, which is supposed to be infinitely compassionate and capable of ushering healing from suffering. Pure Light is supposed to have infinite intelligence; however Pure Darkness also have infinite intelligence.

❖ Vacuum or Black Holes, which are like mostly empty spaces.

❖ Turbulent Waves, which are energy forms that are left behind from certain occurrences there. They may feel like the Aurora Borealis or even strong stormy waves in the sky.

The pie chart in figure 1. gives a rough estimate of the percentages of occurrence of energy and matter in the universe.

Figure 1: Contents of the Universe

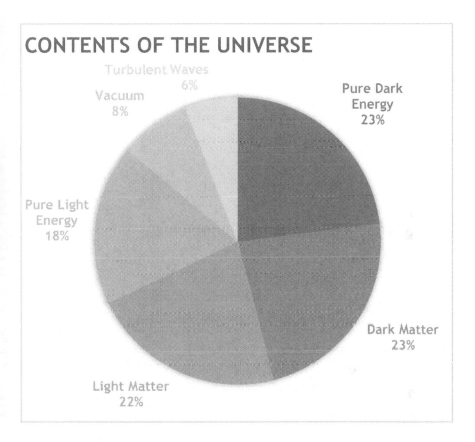

I added this chapter after I had finished most of the book. So, when I started drawing the pie chart, I saw a consciousness appear, who seemed to represent the Pure Dark Energy. He said, "We also have infinite intelligence. We aren't against you." I noticed that his energy was of that of Darkness, which sends chills down the spine. I did not speak but I felt hope and wanted to know more, so he added, "We also believe in justice. In our part of the Universe, in general, good things happen to good people and bad things happen to bad people."

In my mind, I was wondering what the Dark Elements were. He read my mind and answered, "The Dark Elements are the planets and people just like in the stars." I inferred that his part of the Universe is similar to the stars and planets known to star people except that we are powered by the light and that they are powered by darkness powers.

A day later, I met benign Darkness, and felt that the powers had compassion. Now that I am thinking, I had never felt that kind of compassion in the presence of Light. I have received a lot of healing in the presence of light before, but the usherer of healing seem detached and unmoved; the healing feels warm and relieving inside one's heart and body but the source from which the healing comes, seem apathetic. I felt that when being healed by benign Darkness powers, the warmth is not generated within, but comes from the source of healing and healing happens just fine, it is just very different in experience though similar in results.

I edited the percentages of the pie chart in fig.1 and the content of the bullet points in the first paragraph, after having a firsthand conversation with some of the Dark Element kings and mercenaries.

"The Dark Element kings do not like being discussed by humans so do not discuss or write about them on the internet or

anywhere. This is good for your health." said a king of a few
planets from a part of the Dark Matter Universe.

The above photograph depicts the Kailash Mountain in the background. The rectangular fire pit is known as a Havan Kund, where people pray to the fire god Agni. The man sitting by the fire pit is a yogi meditating by counting the "Rudraksh Mala" over and over again. Such yogis are called a "Katahwa Sadhu". The Rudraksh Mala is made up of the dried seeds of the Rudraksh fruit, strung together in an endless chain. The Rudraksh beads are considered sacred and treated with respect by the Hindus and the Buddhists.

ASCENSION TO HIGHER DIMENSIONS

There are programs that can help people evolve. Instead of detailed regimen laid out in spiritual scriptures of Buddhism and other Zen cultures, I would say start with leveraging the healing powers of the five elements, air, water, fire, earth and sacred space. The analogy in action being exposing yourself to musical waves, swimming in water, sitting by natural fire with a prayer to cleanse, sleeping or sitting on the ground for at least an hour each day, and meditating into the empty space. Music can come in the form of classical music, Techno, and other forms as well, chimes, bells, tuning fork and the Hathor sistrum. Besides swimming, it helps to do sea salt baths and sit by rapid flowing rivers with large water bodies. Many Shamans do regular Fire Ceremony for releasing repressed emotions and cleansing the Chakras. We come close to Earth via mud baths and walking bare feet on the ground. This discharges the ions collected in the body that are extra or not needed, much like discharging a circuit board through grounding.

Meditation has benefits of opening the mind and broadening your horizon through claircognitive downloads from the divine. The nuggets appear to us as an inkling or intuition, even a daydream. Meditation can help in developing the right as well as the left brain and strengthening the circuitry between them, thus helping us excel in our academics, jobs and expression of our feelings and emotions with more eloquence and purpose.

The ascension teachings are the tools for us to evolve and either get a clear chit back to our star nations or a realm of Light and be free from earthly incarnations but after the repeated star-wars some of the realms of light where ascended people from Earth go and live were obliterated, and so we have a steeper curve towards growing spiritually and awakening our wisdom and compassion within the limits of our full potential.

Other than getting closer to the divine light from which we all sprang, ascension brings freedom from the cycle of human birth and a place in our "Lightish" realm where we live a purer version of life, like in an 'Ashram'. The Lightish realms are of people's own religion. For people who identify themselves to be an atheist, a non-denominational Lightish realm exists. The dos and don'ts in these Lightish realms follow the scriptures, the traditional codes of conduct and ethics of livelihood. For people who claim themselves as agnostic, they go to the Lightish of their own religion of birth. People do get judged in their

Lightishes and live accordingly. The popular saying that goes like, "God doesn't judge you.", is not true. In the end it does not matter who you were, life will judge you on the basis of your deeds or karma, regardless of your race, money, education or the lack of it.

We stop incarnating on Earth after ascension to the fifth dimension in terms of our wisdom, compassion, cleared chakras and kundalini awakening which is a terminology from Oriental understanding of ascension or Moksha or Nirvana. Very rarely, humans who have ascended to the fifth dimension also incarnate on Earth usually for leading others into goodness and virtue.

The Hathors had started evolutionary teachings through various cults and religions such as those of the Buddhists, the Sufis, the Mithras, the Sakyas, the Tibetans. They have worked through various people who are famous as spiritual masters who were channeled teachings to propagate to people for their spiritual growth.

Most spiritual books that have star content have been celebrated for coming from the stars, but a handful have caused societal issues due to information that were lost in translation. I found out that the scriptures of the Lamas from the 14th century says that the Hathors said that the more often you sleep with women, the quicker you will attain 'Nirvana' or ascension. The person, who had channeled that, was a Hathor vagabond on Earth, and had channeled that to the Tibetan Buddhist monks of

Samye monastery. The women that were dragged into this received nothing in exchange, except for infamy and abuse even at the hands of family members who had to live through the rumors. This led to slavery of women which escalated into no marriages in the society other than for the king and his closest family members. A 14th century ghost of a Panchen Lama from the Gelug school of Tibetan Buddhism says that they were taught: "The more women, the more power. The more you get intimate with a woman, the more power you draw from a certain divine relic." Much later I found out that the Tibetans are a type of Hathor minority race that the Hathor vagabonds who were of a different sub-race, were preaching them to break down their society, due to hatred they had harbored due to memories of past battles over land and resources.

In the path to ascension, energy healing speeds things up, it is like vitamin supplements over your regular meals and exercise. Energy healing works on raising people's body frequencies only to the extent of removing debris, denser foreign blocks of energy and healing and elevating our Chakras of off unresolved grief and repressed emotions thus attaining higher states of awareness, but it does not help in refining people's own souls. The personal dense energies are especially existent among people who don't like to "talk" and go through life on a treadmill without pausing to reflect or think from a different point of view or by stepping into someone else's shoes. Therefore, ascension is not about clearing the body of debris but refining one's own energy to higher frequencies of compassion, wisdom, forgiveness and understanding. The soul energy gets refined over time through various incarnations where people have experienced different roles under varying situations enabling experience of a wide range of emotions and a chance to exercise giving to people even when someone did not have enough.

In Shamanic lore, a "Power Animal" is a Divine consciousness who helps mortals in dire circumstances when they are thrown aboard way against who their soul is and what they can achieve. They bring divine means for getting help to mortals, keeping them alive till their predestined time. They come and go out of our lives on their own. Shamans do retrieve them for people, but they are considered an extra help like the icing on a cake.

CHAPTER III

THE BIGGER PROBLEMS OF EARTH

Photo by Sarita Gupta, taken in January 2013, at St. Augustine, FL

THE MAKE-POSSIBLE-RS' BREWS

The star-wars aren't all lies, so it is good to know that star people exist and that some of the star-wars have brought devastation to Earth either because they took place on Earth or Earth's resources were stolen or mutated or Earth was directly attacked. Some of these wars were fought for political gain in terms of access to Earth's resources, and some for avengement so Earth hasn't been at the receiving end of kindness from the folks with higher levels of evolution.

Earth has had its benefactors in the stars. There are stars like Arborra, Obalesk, Sirius, Beut, Tau Ceti, Mirastar, the Sun, and planets Venus and Saturn, that have helped this planet and us in various ways over time.

The "Gods" and "Goddesses" are star people and light-beings who have helped us in the past. By light-beings here, I mean benign star people who are usually from very ancient stars that might be dead or have just moved on from incarnating into ordinary lives and exist in a more etheric realm living life with more discipline and trying to bring peace and justice around themselves, if they can. The "deities" are more prevalent among the polytheistic religions such as Hinduism, and less among the monotheistic religions such as Christianity, and other Abrahamic religions, where we pray to God as one almighty power which in spiritual understanding would be a divine hologram where the divine is the source of light from which we all sprang.

The "Gods" and "Goddesses" still brew. They have tweaked the astronomical and astrophysical dimensions and other geophysical configurations of Earth over time to suit the impending needs. Some of the tweaking they did were to suit their own needs politically and personally which has affected us adversely. This especially happened after the Gods got angry, which in spiritual understanding would mean that they got nothing out of humanity after working for them for a long time, and also that they also have political enemies in the stars who have attacked them and subsequently attacked Earth. Our planet is just like a country in the bigger arena of the Outer Space and there are other "countries" who don't like us or consider us as enemy. Earth is at a perilous place today, astrophysically, genetically and catastrophically.

Like every other planet or constellation, Earth also has enemies in the stars, and so these people indirectly regulate the scientific experiments, research, DNA mutations and nuclear activity on Earth in lieu of threats of earthquakes and landslides and other seemingly natural disasters. The enemies of Earth also play with the Moon's configuration to change the gravitational pull of Earth to regulate water levels and the Sun's configuration to regulate temperature. Since the water level changes are easily achieved, the star people use it regularly to blackmail certain geographically afflicted governments into doing whatever they want at that time.

Earth has been attacked by Earth-hater and humanity-hater star nations in the last two decades. There have been man-made Tsunami, avalanche, landslides and slow turbulence in the beds of the oceans and subsequent rise in the water levels which are projected to cause flooding in certain areas of the shores.

The stars also influence our research work funded by the bigger agencies as such as DARPA or NASA and the larger medical companies. They also guide the astronomers and the Space Cadets in their inventions sometimes positively but sometimes I have noticed that they allow the humans to spend money on research and then thwart the results or guide the papers erroneously at the very last moment. I wondered if they did it to satisfy their latent sadism especially because I know that those papers were initially going in the right direction of the truth. Then I heard from them that it is easier to curb at the last moment than from the beginning to end. As an example you would find many research papers start very well and you think you would find something meaningful in the end that you can learn as something new or find something useful to apply in your project or invention, but then you see that towards the end of the paper when about two paragraphs are left it takes a downward turn almost refuting what it started with and not revealing anything new. I learnt that the people who do this are light-beings as well as star people who are the enemies of the Hathors. Sometimes even the Hathors are asked by their enemies or some other people trying to maintain a certain inter-galactic standard to curb a certain research, this being especially true in the case of explorative astronomy.

The food industry is controlled by the light kingdoms and the stars. The genetic changes to grow more food was initially well intended but then greed seeped in and the plans took a turn and things grew out of control. Then the organic food industry was developed after light couldn't keep up the fight over quality food with darkness. Reviving organic food was a great idea in a country that isn't agriculture heavy anymore. Recently the composition of soda has been changed and also of other beverages. The Outer Space has been threatening owners of the food industry into working in Darkness against Earth in lieu of their stocks holding their price on the Wall Street. They have brought chemicals from the stars on Earth which are stored in the invisible realms and used against food, beverages and people, as an when they need to attack.

CDMA has proved to be bad for us. It is used in conjunction with other rays at a certain frequency to create terror in the minds of the humans when bombarded at certain receptors of the nervous system. They use this to terrorize people in influential positions to corner them into acting in a certain way to achieve a desired result. This has affected the hospitality industry quite a bit where they have used it successfully into terrorizing guests into leaving. Different star people have different understanding of what a society should enable, and some do not like people making money, travelling or eating out, and they have power and they spend it, they don't strategize much. There are people who strategize and those are the Time Machine builders. But they invite lame haters too who work against us, just differently.

A lot of damage has happened, since the 1960s as a result of the DNA mutations by the order of the Darkness realms. Some of these happened by the order of star people who wanted to mess with humans and some of it were carried by those who could hear clairaudiently such as people from the secret societies.

The Illuminati, the free masons and others secret societies usually have clairaudience and some of them are promised election wins, higher positions in their organizations, more money, or some gig, and are asked to ruin Earth and humanity which they do. Some people who are already accomplished on their own like emperors and CEOs and even authors are approached and threatened into following orders that are not in the best interests of humanity. The kind of people who are threatened instead of promised goodies are the ones who would be considered pious. This is because Darkness goes by what would work safely because they don't want to catch attention of the light. So, they bribe greedy people and threaten the pious. When people with integrity are bribed, they think twice and mull over the righteousness of such an act, and so in this process they connect with the light trying to validate the morality of it and so light catches attention and some light-beings comes to thwart the efforts of Darkness. However, Darkness doesn't mind threatening good people because then they are declaring an open war versus being squelched surreptitiously by the light.

The make-possibler's brews led to new autoimmune diseases, newer personality disorders, DNA mutations targeted to control the minds of people to their detriment, messing with government documents, messing with the familial structure through introducing targeted non-humanoid creatures in the mix of the souls at the time of our birth and DNA mutations to break down familial ties so that people suffer silently in their lives. The unwillingness to pay child support or taking care of children was not a desired change but a byproduct of the desired change of lowered ability to connect with women and need to use them as means for entertainment and financial gains. This resulted into lower marriage rates among monogamous couples and higher number of live births in America to unmarried parents.

For the "developing countries" those DNA mutations resulted in men wanting women to get out of the house and get a job so that they could add to their household income, and the fathers not wanting to marry off their daughters because they think if they remained unmarried they would be the Golden

Goose and be tied to the birth family forever to serve. So, the developing countries actually gained indirectly, by having increased number of women in the workforce without a women's reform movement, but the daughters suffered because of the increased paternal dysfunction. This is because they were treated inferiorly growing up, for being a woman and so they could never step up to that plate of expectations because they couldn't literally transform themselves to a man. They also had this expectation of growing up to be a good wife for someone but at the same time the search for approval from the father never ended because in adulthood they had to go get a job and routinely hand over their wages to their fathers hoping to feel that acceptance they never felt in childhood and for the fathers the incoming income kept them from allowing the daughters to marry and so the daughters couldn't even have a man in their lives, and so they had a yet different problem in adulthood which had to do with realizing themselves without a man, which in childhood was just about finding their place as a woman but in adulthood had doubled up to finding their place in society as a woman and without a man.

LEGERDEMAIN FROM THE STARS

Most of the recent star-wars are wars between computer programs that feed into huge holograms or supercomputers comprised of the powers of Light, Alchemy, Darkness and the Elements of various stars. For the computer savvy, people have written input-output model-based software against the Solid-State circuitry that they have built using various star products that are natural as well as man-made.

The actual laws of Physics permitted by that gigantic hologram of light powering the universe of incarnate star people including us, remain constant but the constants of Physics were altered to create malevolently desired aberrations and other resultant energetic phenomena. For example, the constants of Physics were changed by changing Earth's magnetic core, tilt, and the molecular structure of the stratosphere which bounces back electromagnetic waves for radio communication. In a layman's terms, you could think of the star attacks that do not involve interacting with people, as bad wireless and other invisible technologies used to deform normal situations and things at the will of the attackers.

As part of Biological warfare, aberrations or mutated forms were created in the nuclei, atoms and molecules of various organisms and substances to bring forth desired mutated effect within people's bodies and to cause environmental pollution.

The refractive index of water, and the rainbow colors were changed. The rainbow colors were changed by changing the composition of light infiltering Earth's atmosphere. This was achieved by changing the composition of light being emitted out of the Sun by changing the configurations of the Sun.

As part of the legerdemain employed in the recent starwars, even the interactions with people were programmed to cause desired, controlled negative interactions between specific people. So, everything is programmed and invisible and malevolent, that happened behind the scenes and exists on Earth and on some stars and have been affecting our daily lives in ways that are trending worse than before. In the past, such as 20,000 years ago when Earth was as much hated and attacked as now, the use of chip technology was negligent and it was just Darkness powers sorcering elemental powers, and Light powers also sorcering elemental powers against people and it was mostly like a bar fight among people with very little organized, streamlined, Control Room managed, warfare which even the sponsors of it don't know how to dismantle when they think they could call it good. You can imagine it to be like the game of Quake in a network mode, where different participants have different armors and powers and they all are set to defend themselves or die eventually. So, about a millionth of the soul of each of the humans have been etched out of their bodies and these soul parts are the characters in that megalithic quake-like game which does not end. Once the soul-parts die, they are resurrected and built up similarly, just that in the next game their fate is different because of the heuristics of the Artificial Intelligence of the game itself and the inputs into the megalithic structure that supports and runs that game. The setup appears as a series of guerilla attacks, but it is all controlled by a previously designed model and the data inputs while the system is running, the data being the reactions of people while they are being attacked.

These all sound like I am a gamer but the last game I have played is Age of Empires in 2005, and the above stories are as real as it can get.

The Earth-hater star people have used the dead, the soul-parts of living humans, and that of the flora and fauna as guinea pigs in their research experiments designed to serve them. They have used chips and other technologies to take over minds of about a couple hundred key people to bring political and economic reforms that are geared towards satisfying a certain agenda laid down by certain star administration, darkness realms and light realms. They have even played with the human DNA. They have carried experiments leading to human Genome problems causing diseases like autism, epilepsy, rheumatoid arthritis, Attention Deficit Disorder (ADD), Celiac disease, type 1 diabetes and other autoimmune diseases. Multiple Sclerosis was a side effect of the Biological warfare on humanity.

They have also used Time Machines quite rampantly. The Time Machines contain different realms which share their spatial axes coexisting in the same space, like two containers superimposed in the same space on the axis of time. In this case people do not collide or interact with each other, unless they share the same token of time. This is done to create time slices of events within a particular space, so you can think of it as a time machine inside a room where you hop on and go to the past and hop off and come back to the present. More axes and features are added to such Time Machines to accomplish more. Another version of the Time Machine would have different vertices but share the same superimposed space, with each container having its own time axis. The time machines are used to keep certain havocs going over a long time because it can warp the time axis using reverse and cyclic time spans, stopping the flow of the Universal laws of Physics.

Photo by Sarita Gupta, taken in June 2019.

The Tibetan Wheel of Time is powered by Sirius. It started as a Wheel of Life. It used to be powered by the light, and the magic of the Elements and the supernaturals of Tibet. Then in the 16th century, Sirius took over the Tibetan spiritual realms and artifacts, and restructured their magic to be more scientific. The intentions of Sirius were benign, however, in the last ~600 years, things have changed and the Wheel of Time which had actually become a Time Machine got pushed into darker purposes. The 2012 marker for the end of the World wasn't a myth. The Time Machine was going to explode Earth in 2012. This is because a past king of Sirius and a cousin of a past king of Leutha who had been doing charity work for Earth for about 4500 years, lost more than received in terms of gratitude, honor, monetary gains, political influence and relationships with other star nations and even in terms of accumulating good karma. Some of the decisions that they took at certain times that they had to quite hastily decide being on a running axis of time had backfired, some of which they weren't proud about. About four sentences ago, the past Sirius king had told me that it had gotten personal for him, rather than just being political and therefore he wanted Earth obliterated, however I had shunned away from writing that, but he just now asked me to clarify that here.

Earth hasn't exploded yet because the Hathors wanted Earth to continue. It has been a strife since then. Initially the past king of Sirius was positively impressed with the work of the Hathors towards saving Earth but in 2016 it got more personal for the owner of that Time Machine, negatively, and Earth has been struggling since then.

About a year ago, a star person named Djeuti said:

"Earth haters are here and hate humanity for the right reasons because they do not understand what is good for them. I would like to warn you that your existence will come to an end if you live like kings, showing lack of respect towards authority. There have been times when I tried helping Earth people, but every time I tried, my effort was thwarted by Earth people, by they themselves or by others."

The star people also employ traditional war techniques in the star-wars but almost everything is computerized, and the traditional warfare doesn't reach Earth due to encapsulation of Earth and its atmosphere by a hollow sphere of light barrier.

Upon Earth some of the star people take bodies and minds of key people to pull some important plugs to carry their agenda. They had taken control of the Central Nervous System by chipping and by latching onto the energy meridians to take over our minds to control lives of about a couple hundred key people to bring political reforms that are geared towards lowering living standards and introducing Communistic traits in Capitalist societies by controlling income, pricing, stock markets, marketing channels and tactics and other socio-economic dynamics. They have also caused smaller disruptions which aren't that small but mess with people's lives, such as causing internet outage for days and months, by the use of large Solid State shields with magnetic properties to deflect the internet signals away so that the signals remain suspended in the air in a distorted shape thus blocking them from reaching the antenna receiver outside the house.

The star people also leverage Earth's Darkness realms and also bring people from the Dark Universe here in return for money and other goodies that they promise to them. The Dark Universe has powers that work easier with the human bodies for taking control of the energy meridian centers or Chakras and running people's lives and so star people leverage them a lot against humanity. They also bring soul-parts of living people from the Third World, who in ghost reality obviously don't need a passport to come to America, who are more than willing to work against us and use them against us.

Asking for light from the Divine for sinister purposes is always denied. Real light does not provide power for crime that is against divine will or the natural flow of the life force of the Universe. The individual soul light of billions of soul-parts of creatures were fused together, spirtually, in servitude, to create a light furnace like a charged lattice of energy in the form of a powerhouse. This powerhouse was used for the purposes of Dark Alchemy. Then they tortured certain people to a certain form where they look non-humanoid with more round eyes, and stunted stature with almost robotic features and mannerism, with vestigial cognitive functioning, numbed emotions with very simple scale of understanding, expectations of truth from others, having a naiveté about themselves, and they do not lie and are devoid of cunning. These people were then tethered to work against whatever to cause all sorts of calamities. The only reason Earth exists is because Earth does have a star administration governing us and several other benefactor light kingdoms and star nations who have invested in humanity in the past who still care and want things to improve if that is a possibility.

An Archaic man who is from a light realm and used to help in healing people and bringing positive change said:

"Humanity has deteriorated over the last sixty years to a place of no love or respect with families and neighbors.

I am at a place where I don't know where to begin. I had friends who believed in goodness and virtue. They are all missing."

Sometimes negative work is done using the elemental powers of the mountains or the oceans and they do not have to obey divine will just like us. Bigger calamities have been achieved artificially such as an earthquake or a landslide using collected light from millions of souls interlaced with elemental powers of the tress and the mountains. For example, the Kaikoura earthquake with magnitude 7.8 that took place in New Zealand on September 14th, 2017 was created using light of the soul of about a million humans from Peru.

THE CONSTANTS OF PHYSICS AREN'T ALWAYS SAME

S tar people who wanted to attack Earth and couldn't just grab people and beat them up, came up with convoluted methods of making us suffer. So, they used pseudoscience which is actually a more advanced Science.

The actual laws of Physics permitted by that gigantic hologram of light powering the light part of the Universe remain constant, but the constants of Physics change according to the field in which we are. The elements of the matter and light in which we are and from which we are observing, both changes the constants. Therefore, when the plane of observation stays constant, a particular constant of Physics changes as a function of the elements of the medium and the light waves that are emitted from those elements as well as the light waves being bombarded at those elements. This can be represented as:

Equation 1.: Constant i = Constants i * f(x), where x defines the medium in which the constant applies to, for a particular law of Physics.

Similarly, when the plane of observation is moving through various medium and the medium in which the constant of a law of Physics is observed, is assumed to remain same, then we can represent that

Equation 2.: Constant i = Constants i * f(y), where y defines the medium of the observer.

Equation 1. effects the mathematical calculations of things where in known Physics, for simplicity, it is assumed that the constants stay constant when in reality they don't always remain same because of the reasons I would be describing in the subsequent paragraphs. Thus Equation 1 is for calculation; this is not for experiencing from outside the zone of wherever things are taking place.

Equation 2. is not for the calculation of the actual energetic occurrences governed by certain laws of Physics, but for observing the phenomenon from a distance. Even when the phenomenon is same in a particular environment what we observe changes based upon from where we are observing. This is due to the translation of properties of one medium with respect to another, the most basic translation being the equation governing the magnetic properties of the mediums. Therefore, considering the properties of wherever we are observing from as a function of y, f(y) where y defines the environment from which we are observing, and the properties of the medium where the constant is being measured as a function of x, f(x), where x defines the medium, then there exists a relationship between f(y) and f(x).

Some people from the Outer Space, altered the properties of molecules by creating polymers and aggregates targeted to make us suffer. Such forms of attacks existed but not at a large scale where it can affect a whole set of measurements to buckle things up, such as creating faults and rifts through the land and the mountains. About half of the earthquakes in the last three years were induced from above.

Some of the malevolently induced aberrations and subsequent change in some of our Physics are described in the flowing p-paragraphs. Star people have changed Earth's magnetic core in certain areas to mess with the gravitational forces to reduce longevity of tall buildings. Now someone would wonder why they just won't make them fall off. A past king of Sirius said, "It is not easy to impart that kind of force through the energetic barriers protecting Earth, but the slow seeping harm can be introduced and has been introduced, in some places of Earth."

Planck's constant was changed which changed the resonance of objects in the effected medium. This was used in conjunction with altered Doppler Shift to cause avalanches.

More about this is explained in the chapter "The 'Natural' Disasters".

Atmospheric pressure was altered and is lesser than before by 10 percent. This has changed several constants of the laws of Physics. For example, in fluid dynamics, the Mach number which is the ratio of flow velocity past a boundary to the local speed of sound has changed so airplanes fly slower than before. This is not really evident but has added about a five minute more in the air time.

The molecular structure of the stratosphere which bounces back electromagnetic waves for radio communication was changed to affect the speed of sound and other constants governing the electromagnetic laws of Physics. The Boltzmann constant (kB) has changed which causes altered electromagnetic induction. This has caused several instances of radio frequency interference due to coupling of noise through some of the radio waves.

AUTISM

sperger's Syndrome was introduced into humanity by the Atmel star in the 1960s. It was politically ordered from the Outer Space for our technological growth. A select group of people were chosen, who were relatively intelligent from before, and their brains were restructured to be able to do more detailed, scientific, research work and complicated mathematical computations. Their Random Access Memory part of the brain was strengthened and the neurological connections to the left brain were drawn from the right brain, thus enhancing their Intelligence Quotient (IQ) which unfortunately came at the cost of reduced emotional intelligence or Emotional Quotient (EQ). This resulted in their social skills being severely impaired with repetitive behavior and reduced set of interests. Atmel said that the reduced set of interests was by design to make people focus on their tasks so that they can excel in their jobs and not wander their minds onto other things that would take their time away from their main jobs.

In the 60s and the 70s Atmel invested in Earth by helping with the invention of chips by taking over the minds of engineers and scientists thus inventing the Atmel Microchip collections in the 1960s. This led to the invention of the Mainframe Supercomputers, the rest is history. They continued inventing chips and strengthening the Solid State technology to bring us access to a PC for individual use. They invested in the growth of the software Industry worldwide with separate branches pioneering in Hungary and Ireland. They helped in bringing the information technology revolution, in return for about 0.005 percent of the intelligent male population from Earth as indented labor whereby they take some soul-parts of each of them to Atmel and there they work for them. In the 70s they were their low wage workers with free housing and food and a salary. Since the 90s, the "converted" people have been working there for free because their investments in humanity were more than what they recuperated. They have continued to "aspergate" people over time, based on their own needs and needs of Earth. In return, on Earth, the "converted" people have gotten Asperger's Syndrome and excel in their engineering job and someone eventually marries them for their money. So, they have an ok life. For the record, Asperger's Syndrome is not a natural disability, it is an attack in the sense that it is a surgery upon us without our permission to herd our life into a certain mold of being.

I had asked Atmel about a year ago about why they choose only men and not women. They said, "We do not want to deal with women. In our culture men go to work. Women stay at home and work and raise family." I asked if all women have families to raise there. They replied, "In our culture all women marry." Their society is more like a Communist society where people have to follow set of government laws in their social lives too otherwise, they get incarcerated.

Atmel provided genetic material for this change in the brain. These people were groomed by them to be computer scientists and hardware engineers, since according to them humans were not that intelligent by the standards of requirement for bringing the Technology Revolution in the world. Atmel held this view; they still hold this view. They just now appeared to me and said that a human brain cannot remember formulae and details of an entire mathematical derivation of a theorem or a lemma to reproduce them at a test examination, however they can.

Atmel chipped the people with Asperger's Syndrome to track them and help them in their success to help humanity succeed. The side effects of being chipped were compromised amygdala leading to abnormalities in the lower order emotional processing of input from sensory receptors causing the observed lack of empathy among people with Asperger's Syndrome, which manifests itself as reduced ability to relate to others, compulsive lying, inappropriate social interaction, poor eye contact, poor understanding of others' feelings, and constant need for adulation.

According to Koscik's paper on Neuropsychologia, "human amygdala is necessary for developing and expressing normal interpersonal trust." Koscik says that the amygdala is involved in extracting trustworthiness information from faces. People with unilateral damage to the amygdala display extra generosity with their money and they tend to increase trust in response to betrayals. Koscik's paper says that neurologically normal adults tend to repay trust in kind, decreasing interpersonal trust in response to betrayals or increased trust in response to fidelity. I have known a person with Asperger's closely, who in my observation, couldn't tell apart a friend from a foe, even though he was intelligent at genius levels and was a software architect.

Spiritually speaking, the people with Asperger's Syndrome gather attention from the ghosts and the star people and also the soul-parts of the living. The reason for this happening is that the inflicted person's head does not function like it is supposed to and so the spiritual aura emanating from the person's Crown Chakra which tells the rest of the universe about who they are and what they are up to is distorted and so other people perceive them as crooked, literally, I mean the head is already crooked after all those chips and non-invasive star surgery, and so the ghosts inflict negativities upon them that are less than deserving of them. Initially, Atmel tried to protect the "Aspies" from the invisible people messing with their heads because they were the cream of the crop among the engineers and the scientists working in the computer industry, but they couldn't keep up with the rising curiosity of many star people and so they had to take a back seat. Then the darker light realms utilized the chips and circuitry in the heads of the people with Asperger's to create lesions and wire more circuitry around, to mess with the "chosen" person, giving rise to the comorbidity of other conditions such as Tourette Syndrome, low functioning symptoms on the spectrum of autism, and other developmental problems.

In 1983, Atmel got an order from one of their upper association leaders to mutate some of the alleles of the people with Asperger's Syndrome for them to become more outgoing and more professing of their emotional feelings for other people. They carried this order out. Some of those genetic changes were inheritable and so their children inherited those DNA, but the children weren't on the "gifted" or super-intelligent spectrum of Aspergers but only on the autistic end of it which is like being mentally challenged. This is because they only had a version of the genetic changes of their parents, but they weren't chosen to be aspergated. The children that were chosen to be aspergated had become super-intelligent like their father and were higher on the autism spectrum. Atmel starts aspergating chosen people only at age ten and sometimes as early as age five. Anyone less than ten, diagnosed with Asperger's are usually progeny of one of the people initially chosen to be aspergated. It has been observed that in some cases the condition had gotten worse down the family tree chain, from son to grandson and so on. The reason for this is to do with unfortunately poor genetic selection and the presence of other genetic diseases running in the family. The daughters in the hereditary chain were also affected but the alleles chosen to be mutated are less significant in the random selection process for a female offspring. People with Asperger's retired okay and eventually died but their progeny suffered most.

The only way to cure Asperger Syndrome for the progeny of those people who were attacked by the darker light realms is by working on the DNA of that family chain and fixing it for them. This is very hard to do in our physical reality. The Atmel star tried to bring a positive change on Earth. It is the dead people working in the darkness realms meddling with the material makings of the world who are to be blamed.

A proof-reader asked me about what this chapter could bring to people, giving example of a friend that I know who has a twenty-three-year-old son who has autism. His father had Asperger's Syndrome and was a software architect who was good at his job. I replied, "This would bring closure to people. She could find it easier to move on and do something different with her life." I knew she spent most of her life taking care of her son and worrying about him and spent about 70 percent of the time describing his problems each time I met her over drinks or food. Then I added, "He would know the real roots of his problems and figure oh this is just some allele problem and try harder at life to overcome those than feel helpless or caged in by a condition." It isn't hard to train the mind to outgrow genetic diseases. Hope is the best medicine we need.

THE NATURAL DISASTERS

Humanity hasn't correlated the roots of its bigger problems to the havoc and goodness brought down from the stars and the politics with the Outer Space.

Seventy-five percent of the "natural" disasters such as land slides, earthquakes, volcanic eruptions and tsunamis were fully generated by star people or at least an existing weak spot or a volcanic hotspot were manipulated to induce them.

Well known problems such as Ozone layer depletion and Global Warning has its roots in the Outer Space. The effects of "Global Warming" are real, which is the rise in the water levels, however the water levels are not higher due to "Global Warming" which the media correlates to be the rise in temperature. Some of the real causes of the rise in the water levels are:

❖ Distance from the Moon

- ❖ Gravitational pull of the Moon
- ❖ Changes in the molecular structure of water
- ❖ Change in the refractive index of water

Some star people take over human bodies fully by kicking out the human soul and fully integrating themselves into the chakras of that body to function as their own. These are not star-seeds that were born as a baby with an alien soul but star people who are strategically placed in a human body by their government to ruin us. This has been happening routinely in the last 10,000 years. Attacks led by them are hidden from our physical eyes and only show up as earthquakes, tsunamis, landslides, effects of Global Warming, flooding, irradiation with harmful rays from the Outer Space and other "natural" disasters or meteorites hitting Earth.

Those who are wondering that natural disasters would require tremendous powers and a star person, even if they had powers worth ten times a human, they will not be able to move a piece of mountain to cause a landslide or break the magma layers to cause a volcanic eruption. That is true. The work is done by a machine-like system built with laser beams, Elemental powers, certain stolen light powers and powers of Darkness They also pool in the light of the souls of humans and tether them into forced action like a cog in a wheel to operate gigantic systems that can initiate the natural disasters. Since these harness of powers fueling the calamity bringing "machines" are *not* divine, they are slave to the commands of whoever owns it. They are not compassionate, justice bringing and constructive but are used for destructive purposes.

The principle of Doppler Effect was exploited to strike resonance with the mountains to cause landslides and avalanches,
by altering the frequency of sound of the winds blowing over
the mountains to match up to the resonating frequency of the
mountains. This was achieved by changing the medium through
which the winds travel. Doppler Effect is best illustrated with
the example of the siren of the horn of a car blowing continuously at a constant, emitted frequency from the horn, but the
perceived pitch or frequency of sound increasing with respect to
a stationary point to where the car is approaching because while
in motion the waves of the sound emitted by the siren gets
squished so the wavelength gets shortened as the car approaches the stationary point and so the sound rises up in pitch,
as per the relationship between wavelength and frequency being
an inverse of each other.

When the medium of travel or the air is normal the winds
do exhibit a doppler effect whereby the pitch of sound increases
as the wind approaches the mountains, but they almost never
reach the resonating frequency to cause any shaking of the
mountains. But the medium or the air or space near the mountains were changed by showering them with patterned laser
beams from the stars and also changing the atmospheric composition through which sound would travel, so the speed and
frequency of sound was different when it blew towards the
mountains so that the mountains could resonate with the regular winds over them, causing them to buckle under resonance.
For the laymen, resonance is the rapid vibration of an object, induced by the ripple effects carried through the air from another
object in its vicinity which is vibrating at its safe limits of opera-
tion. It is like a matchstick striking fire. The air near the

mountains need to be vibrating at a certain frequency for the episode of resonance to kick in and once that happens, it starts vibrating at a very high frequency which cumulates into a state that the mountains are not designed to withstand, causing its collapse or even explosion into an avalanche, depending upon how fast it is shaking. Bridges also usually collapse due to striking resonance with sustained strong winds. Once oscillating in resonance mode, the object cannot be kicked out of resonance unless there is an inbuilt mechanism there to change its resonating frequency from within, for example, the Taipei 101 tower relies on a 660-ton pendulum which acts like a tuned mass damper to modify the response at resonance, by modifying the natural frequency of the tower itself.

Doppler Shift is further explained through the diagrams in Figure 1. and Figure 2, on the next page.

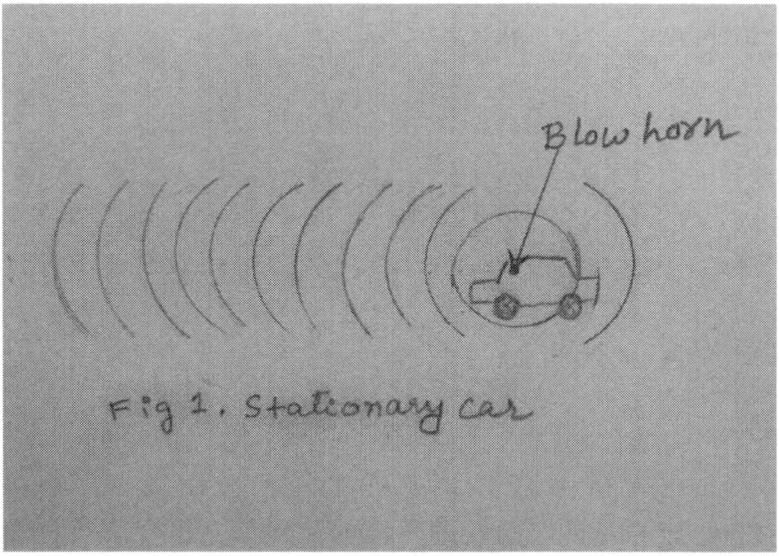

Fig 1. Stationary car

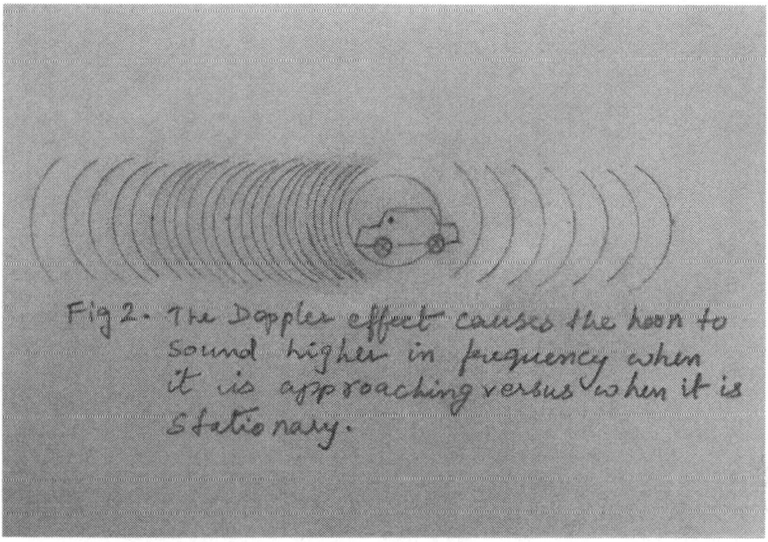

Fig 2. The Doppler effect causes the horn to sound higher in frequency when it is approaching versus when it is stationary.

Without the manipulated Doppler Shift, the winds over the mountains would not push them into resonance mode which have caused about half of the landslides across the globe in the last 30 years. Before that the occurrence of manipulated land-slides were only about 10 percent of the total. In the order of number of occurrences in the last thirty years, most of the ava-lanches and landslides that occurred as part of a star attack, were in Greenland, Alaska, Japan, Chile, Peru and the Himalayas.

In a local experiment upon Earth with the help of a star person from among the star rulers of Earth, I have witnessed altered Doppler ratio using a torrent of laser rays, projecting downwards from above, dancing at random angles, dispersing the molecules of air which also introduced injected light particles, in unison thereby changing the acoustic properties of the medium through which sound travels. This was carried out at a larger scale over targeted mountains to cause presumably natural disasters.

Sometimes negative work is done using the elemental powers of the mountains or the oceans and they do not obey divine will as much as us who have souls made up of divine light. Calamities have been achieved artificially as such as an earthquake or a landslide using collected light from millions of souls of creatures, interlaced with elemental powers of the tress and the mountains. For example, the Kaikoura earthquake of magnitude 7.8 that took place in New Zealand on September 14th, 2017 was created using light of the soul of about a million humans from Peru. I learnt that this disaster was caused by extra-terrestrial mercenaries who were hired by Earth-hater nations. A landslide was induced subsequently by the earthquake. The earthquake was induced by tumult in the magma layer caused by Earth spirits and some other serpents borrowed from the stars. Though the casualties were not many the land areas that were affected were massive.

On December 17th, 2017, there was a landslide in Chile, which was caused by a certain group of mercenaries from a foreign star nation, who had attacked Chile in retaliation to prior attacks upon Peru where they have their base. There a few different groups of mercenaries and sometimes their interests collide, which sometimes results into disasters on Earth. People think that the disasters are caused due to natural mechanisms but that isn't true. This was done using the powers of the Peruvian Mountains and other elemental powers and darkness powers of a few star nations. They used lever-action to crack the tip and break some portions off of the hills. The prime mercenary had lived on Earth, in Peru, for six-hundred years, so he was protecting it from devastation and trying to make a statement for the mercenaries from the stars who have a base in Chile, to back off from attacking Peru.

The landslide in the Cusco region of Peru, on 15th of March 2018, which destroyed more than a hundred houses thus rendering them ininhabitable, was caused by the other star mercenaries, who leveraged powers from the invisible realms of Earth. The news report states that the local authorities have stated that the landslide was caused by "high pore water pressures" which would suggest that the landslide was caused by natural means of activities underneath the Earth's crust. People who don't know more than what meets the eyes, settle into thinking that these were natural disasters, not that they have an option, but I am throwing light on some of the hidden truth.

The Black Snow in Siberia on February 15, 2019 was due to the Sun dumping toxic waste on Earth. Siberia is the part of Earth to which the Sun has direct access. Other parts of Earth are not so accessible due to the Moon and other smaller asteroids and planets in the solar system. This waste seems harmful, but that part of Siberia is considered uninhabited as compared to the rest of the Earth by several people from the Outer Space. The Sun king said, "However people do live there but the Sun doesn't have a choice about dumping waste from their own industries." The waste materials here have two sides to it. The cloud over Siberia also protects the Earth from invaders and stays there almost constantly and so the black snow is quite a regular phenomenon in that region. This is not a mercenary act or a criminal act but just that those black rain aren't that natural.

Photo, taken in 6/2019.

The hand-woven drum depicts the photo of a mythical bird.

THE CONDOR IS NOT HAPPY

One evening in August 2018, I was playing a Shamanic drum that I had picked up from a goodwill store. I entered trance like state whereby I could see and hear spirits vaguely. Soon I was greeted by the Lakota tribe's chief. I learnt that the drum was hand woven by his people. A lot of Native American spirits came to help heal my body. A group of people which included dead humans and humanity-hating star nations, attacked the tribe chief's spirit which was a shame.

In November 2018, I was praying looking at the statue of a Condor. A Condor appeared within a minute and offered help. He provided some spiritual healing and brought some good luck to my house. I had never seen a Condor before. I had read about them in a book on Shamanism but hadn't believed that they exist. They are mythical creatures that are quite large in size, of the size of a large ostrich and have a wingspan only second in length to the albatross. They are not visible to the human eye without the aid of clairvoyance. They live in the East, which is an invisible realm, usually on the top of mountains. The Condors live in the valley. In the Quechua language of the Peruvian people, they are called *kuntur* which is where their name is derived from. They are big hearted birds and are symbolic of wisdom and looking at the big picture.

I heard three days later that, that particular Condor was attacked in an extra-terrestrial unrest. A proof-reader asked if those star people can read this and if I should be afraid. Yeah they can read this and I have noticed with some of the enemies of Earth such as certain types of serpent-people, certain types of saurichia that when we are aware that they are expressing enmity or dislike of us, it calms them a bit as if their hatred was heard and so they only observe rather than attack actively.

The word "Shaman" is actually a Hathor word. The Hathor people are same as the ones who constructed the temple at Dendera in Egypt. They are the star race of the Pharaohs. Most of the Pharaohs and their first wives weren't human and would be considered star-seeds. The "Shaman" word means the one who has attained priesthood. The first shamans on Earth were actually from Siberia. The reason for this is that one of the earliest humans were settled in Siberia ~556,000 years ago, by Neufferseumaat who was the then Hathor queen. Some of those humanoids were taught the ways to awaken themselves into higher levels of thinking and compassion by her and they were called shamans and the tradition carried on over the ages and passed from the Siberians to the Mongolians and made all the way to Alaska and subsequently to the Americas after the Siberians migrated to the Americas via the Bering strait. The Shamanic practices continued since then and died in North America after the Europeans conquered North America. However, the spirits of the Native American shamans live in the Middle World and do possess bodies of their progeny for spiritual healing work and some for just enjoying life beyond death.

Shamanism was restricted to Native American communities until the 1970s when the Hathors popularized it by appearing to probable healers in their trance states and shamanic journeys, introducing themselves to mediums and people with clairaudience, to help them grow into a spiritual healer and to help them with their spiritual healing work to promote awareness of shamanism. They guided people into becoming successful shamanic healers to bring back holistic approaches of medicine into practice. In the last thirty years, several prominent shamanic literature from Peru made its way to us. There are plenty of non-Native shamans available these days who provide shamanic spiritual healing. This was a good revival for the growth of the collective human consciousness.

In spiritual literature a crossroad is a natural place on Earth where there is seclusion from neighboring invisible realms and act like a natural Sacred Space. In Shamanic culture, there is a concept of creating Sacred Space before doing spiritual healing on people. The analogy would be that of a quarantined environment free of germs and mischievous spirits to do healing and surgery work. Shamans and Energy healers create Sacred Space, by drumming, or rattling and some don't drum or rattle but just close their eyes and focus and invoke the guarding spirits through a prayer whereby the call the relevant protective energy holograms and the Directions. In Shamanic tradition, the Directions are each personified as a mythical entity to who we pray directly and each of the directions have their own characteristics and how they influence our lives. The South is considered to be the Great Serpent who can help us shed heavy energy and our past like they shed their skin to renew and bring in new blessings and positivity. The West is personified by the Jaguar who is brings in courage, perfection and cleanliness, the Jaguar being a cleanly animal. The North is personified by hummingbird which helps us adapt easily to situations and make the most of their new circumstances. The East is personified by the Condor. The East is considered the most sacred of the directions and the seat of wisdom where we rise above petty feelings and actions and take a step back to look at the situation with a bird's eye view to understand the entire problem space. For people who do not believe any of the above analogies with the directions can think of it as embracing those qualities and bringing them into our lives by consciously thinking about them and wanting to live a better life.

The Shamanistic cultures had become a target, because we had seen a rise in Shamanic practices in the last three years which could have helped people heal holistically and naturally at a much cheaper price than prevailing medical and surgical treatments. The Shamans bring holistic medicine and Earth-haters did not want Earth people to avail of it. The attackers from among the humans were soul-parts of owners of medical insurance companies, physicians, surgeons, dentists, orthodontists and even plastic surgeons.

THE INVISIBLE LIT-TER

The waste products on Earth have increased since higher dimensional realms have been created on Earth. There are thousands of higher dimensional realms, separated in pockets, within mountains, superimposed upon key people's houses, inside the surface of Earth, and some remote areas. These waste products are not even visible, so humans can't clean them up and star people who are benefitting from them would be ordained to clean them up. Once, a star person with an invisible settlement on Earth who seemed like a nice person, asked politely:

"What is a 'waste'?"

"I mean byproducts of their existence and daily activities and industries that are harmful for the existence of humans and ancient supernatural beings of Earth," I replied passively.

The above mentioned settlements were created by our extra-terrestrial enemies and some of the good people who have those settlements were invited by the enemies of the Hathors. Some of these settlements are occupied by friends of Earth who are helping in cleaning up the mess of unfavorable wirings, spurious or extraordinary technology, and negative people who want to steal Earth's resources and even resources of our benefactors in the stars. Since October 2018, the invisible smog has attracted extra-terrestrials from too many star nations who are here and they each have a different understanding of what is happening for Earth in the invisible reality and they each assume a different understanding of the role of the star rulers of Earth and their work on Earth and want different things from them.

Coming back to waste products that are visible to us, the way they have been compounded have created problems in the atmosphere. The current method of transmuting collected garbage pile leads to poisonous gas polluting the atmosphere. The methods of managing industrial waste need change for long term sustenance of life on this planet. The suggested remedies for waste management are to burn the landfill instead of burying it. This will reduce slow food poisoning through afflicted crops but will cause increased air pollution. The air pollution can be offset by adding certain chemicals while burning and is still a better remedy as compared to burying. People started burying instead of incinerating because they needed fertilizers, but that practice started with burying compost. These days they bury almost all byproducts. Adsorbents as such as activated charcoal can be used around the incinerators to soak up toxins.

Our waking consciousness isn't aware of the spiritual, nuclear wars that occur in our invisible realms and these wars don't have to respect the nuclear treaties and they don't follow them. Some of the nuclear attacks are localized and happen to individuals and some are bigger organized attacks among supernatural beings and people of countries that aren't on friendly terms. The nuclear debris and radiation from the refactors as well as the spiritual warfare are unmanageable and have been causing new forms of diseases, most of which are congenital in nature. People have had the incidents of stunted and deformed bones in adults and babies, weakened capillaries, heart palpitations, loss of smell, and blurry vision. Compared to conventional heavy metals such as Uranium, the molecular structure of the resulting waste from the synthetic radioactive fuels is carcinogenic and have already introduced diseases that will take two to six generations to clear.

The EMF (electromotive force) waste from computers and other devices employing chips needs to be handled by star people, at a large scale. We can't see the EMF radiations, but intuitively use crystals that soak them up. There has been excessive EMF production which are chipping at our systems, over time. This isn't just from the regular networks that we know of, but also from heavy-duty beams that are being projected from the stars, some of which are our inadvertent enemies, and some light that were brought from the star administrators, with the permission of their proprietors. If you could see them, they would look like cobwebs everywhere, in various shapes and sizes and in some targeted places, they would look like a pub where the discotheque balls project beams out in an array of frequencies and directions. In human reality, it doesn't really create detectable problems in the existing networks' functioning or data connectivity between network nodes, but there is too much of invisible infrared and laser networks causing extra amounts of harmful EMF (electromotive force) radiations. I learnt that infrared is made up of elements and rays from some of the Red stars. I discovered that since the year 2017 some of the newer, extra-terrestrial time-machines have been exploring Martian rays to further biological warfare, sometimes upon us.

Lately, there have been a lot of sound pollution which goes undetected. Sound frequencies have been brought down from the stars that act like viruses effecting the wireless signals, our health, and our electronics. There is also supersonic sound that can actually affect us at organ level and can achieve almost anything with our bodies and electronics. They exist and can cause diseases over a period of time. It is like living and stepping through buzzing of all sorts of frequencies for which our bodies aren't designed. Some of the unexpected noise is generated from the friction of motion of UFOs in our environment, and from movements of other beings and artifacts of the invisible realms of Earth. We aren't unaffected by the undetected frequencies of soumd near or within our body.

At this point, cutting down on some of the excessive technologies and living life holistically is a big way to reduce our exposure to the EMF debris, and other harmful radiations causing health issues. Crystals near the electrical and electronics devices also help, especially black, matte rocks. Reducing the use of gadgets and living an active life to sweat out excessive toxin buildups, spending time in sauna, exercise, and getting lymphatic drainage massages would help. Energy healers can help remove the extra EMFs as well. Grounding yourself by spending time barefoot in the grass for at least few minutes a day, would help you to get lasting health.

INVENTIONS LEADING TO CYBECRIME

In the last 4 years laser was fabricated in criminal ways to cause things to buckle up. Prongs, micro and mini "bots" were constructed out of CDMA waves, H900 wireless networks and laser beams and they were used to ruin targeted electronic and mechanical systems. They were also used to ruin foundations of buildings, kill trees, ruin cars, stereos, vacuum cleaners, refrigerators, dishwashers, robotic vacuum cleaners and other electronic equipment.

Laser networks were used to hijack wireless hops to hack secure systems. The breach in security affected me most because I could figure that my emails were accessed such as unread emails showing as read, and attachments missing, and in some cases, altered. Someone had even logged onto my brokerage account and changed my address to theirs. This had caused identity theft issues. It is just that it has gotten way more detailed in how much it can achieve without leaving a footprint.

10,000 years ago, during the reign of the Pharaohs on Earth, there was a debacle that had caused the death of about 25 percent of the population. People had gotten clairaudience and clairvoyance and so people knew each other's lives, secrets, PIIs (personally identifiable information) and it was identity theft at a whole different level of that of robberies, loot, murder, in cavemen style versus on the world wide web.

Recently I have come across extreme cases where people's credit scores have been compromised. Having clairaudience requires accountability just like when you are a in a profession where you have access to people's personal information, but you keep it a secret and don't mess with it.

For some people, the Bluetooth Service was hacked, and new wrappers added onto it and then the hacked service was installed replacing the Bluetooth services that came with the Computer. Subsequently data was accessed and stolen from the computers. This wasn't that rampant before. The software industry needs to secure itself against the new set of hackers.

There have been too many inventions brought down form the stars that mess with our wireless networks not only the high-level networking protocols such a TCP\IP but also the lower level wireless network protocols and so these viruses not only mess with our electronics but also our brains and health.

At this point living life holistically is a good way to be in control of our documents that have been getting accessed and altered on the world wide web. People's emails have been compromised. Several people's attachments were deleted and some altered. Reducing paper was a good campaign to simplify life but going back to paper will counter the identity theft which is widespread.

Photo by Sarita Gupta, taken in 2015, at a Western Washington farm.

CHAPTER IV

SAVING EARTH

Photo by Sarita Gupta, of the obelisk at the Karnak temple, Egypt.

WE ARE GOVERNED BY THE STARS

On Earth we have rulers, presidents, kings and queens and they each govern their dominion, but they don't rule Earth with respect to the Outer Space. In the stars also there are rulers, kings and queens of the denomination of what we know of on Earth, but they all have a ruler for the entire planet who deals with the bigger problems of the planet including interplanetary problems with respect to its neighboring planets. Therefore, Earth as a planet has a star administration.

The Hathor have dominion over some parts of Earth and remaining is governed by the Korean and other star administrations. The Hathors spiritually led the discovery of America in 1492. Our existing literature upon Earth talks about the Hathor people settling parts of Egypt. The literature also talks about the Obelisk, the pillar, which was built with the help of the Obli galactic association and the Hathors. I learnt that the Obelisk in Washington D.C. was built by them.

I discovered that Hathor, pronounced as Hathrr, are a type of a humanoid form which consists of supernaturals from a collection of planets and stars. Some of the Hathors are from Arborra and other stars and planets built, re-built and settled by them. I discovered that the Hathors have also settled parts of Siberia, parts of Nepal, parts of India and parts of the state of Alaska in the United States of America. I learnt from my investigations while space-traveling, astrally and subsequent geophysical analysis of the soil material that the permafrost layer of the Earth's crust in Alaska is made up of one of the Green Hathor clan's soil. A lot of the rocks and some of the precious stones were formed out of resources brought down from various stars and planets under the star administrations of Earth.

The Sun also helps us, but about 1.3 million years ago they needed to cut their losses short after a big, galactic war when the Sun was attacked and had to leave Earth in dearth, in a dormant state after which it was bought by the Red Pharoahs. After the Red Giant star galactic attackers left, slowly the Sun started showing interest in resettling Earth with life. About 800,000 years ago, the Hathor star people were invited by the Sun king to settle Earth. Then the Earth's crust was solidified with the help of technology provided by the Hathors, to make it habitable for the prehistoric animals as well as humans. The resources of the Hathors were used to make and maintain some of the initial human population. Over time, this planet has seen other conquerors who came to Earth with a flag. There were other star people also who came to Earth upon invitation. Thereby this planet has been settled by several star nations.

Earth has been doing better than before in the last thousand years. This is due to the hard work of the benefactors of Earth in the stars. They brought Earth out of the nomadic life to which it had resorted at the bottom of that sinusoidal curve of prosperity and peril, into successive resurgence of the Bronze Age, the Iron Age, the French Revolution, the Industrial Revolution, and the Technological Revolution. However, there has been extra-terrestrial unrest in the last three years and so things have taken a turn on that sinusoidal curve and we are heading downwards. The approximate highs for humanity in the last one thousand years would be the discovery of America, the Moon Landing, the technological revolution, and the revolution in handheld devices.

Lately the scene has changed, and we have been heading downhill.

In the year of 2017, a star person from the Koet galaxy, many lightyears away, remarked:

"Earth has earned a name outside, to very far off places too, of being unruly and out of control with their superiors."

The major problem is that soul-parts of living humans were etched out of their bodies and harnessed into doing organized crime, as well as they were let loose to wander here and there like in an Out-of-Body experience (OOBE) to doing all sorts of vandalism or whatever suited their fancy. This wasn't the case ever before and star people did this. There is no remedy for this at our end because our cognitive minds don't know about it and so we cannot be informed enough before our next alien abduction. They usually target the top two hundred influential people in the world to bring in changes in the laws, influence our politics, our crops, and the world of medicine.

A friend of mine who has proof-read this book, said:

```
"This book should have come to us, pack-
aged in truth like this, a few thousand
years ago."
```

In the last sixteen years, he has been among the top ten humans who routinely get abducted by star people of various star nations. Different people had different things to do with him. The other humans that were most abducted were a handful of famous Hollywood celebrities. The reasons for abduction vary within the purposes of plain curiosity, romance, personal entertainment, incarceration, legal execution, putting them to indented work, using them politically against someone else, and using them as a pawn or a bargain.

When meeting star people, it is important to understand that they are just a different looking version of humans, more technically a supernatural or a higher power humanoid, and not a God. The Gods are star people who have had incarnations on Earth or have lived on Earth for extended periods of time and have helped humanity. It is important that we maintain our own honor as well as respect the star people we may meet. It is important to not expect money or women from them and understand that many could be humanity-haters who may want to abduct us into slavery after we prove to them that we are indeed as bad as they think humans are. It is good to act like there are laws and rules to abide by and we are not in a free-for-all.

When humans meet star people, they act and think like, "What happens in Vegas stays in Vegas." This is not true. They may not be visible to the humans in their waking reality, but they are living people just like us, with jobs, families, money, legal systems, politics, and governments. Humans are advised not to leave Earth, while astral travelling out of their bodies. If you happen to meet star people, perceiving them, audibly or visibly, interact with accountability. Being withdrawn is more advised than being curious or extroverted. Only people with clairvoyance can see the star people, unless in a dream or in a trance like state induced via, self-hypnosis or by the alien trying to establish communication. Most people don't remember the interaction after waking up or getting out of the trance. Treating them poorly or not upholding our own morals, causes collective problem for Earth as a nation and affects its political relationship with the Outer Space.

When I started writing this book, because I could hear, several invisible people came forward to channel whatever they wanted heard. I am going to include a story channeled by a past Korean royalty from ~4780 years ago. It was hard to bring justice even then.

"I was a teenager. I saw a big flame of fire out in the sky. It was like a fiery ball falling on Earth. I ran home and informed my father who was king of Korea then. He said, "Don't worry; it is a comet falling on the Japanese." I felt bad because I had been in Japan when I was about nine and people were kind to me there. An old man had offered me some "Aye-sokee" which is a good luck charm and I had begun to believe that it was bringing me some good luck in my interactions with my peers at the palace. I awaited the news of what catastrophes it created upon the local people there. I did not quite eat that day. Next morning, I asked my father about the news of what happened with that comet. He said "Don't worry son. It did not hit us." Then I asked further and he said, "It killed a lot of people. About a thousand." Then I asked if it hit that town. He said, "The report says that it did hit that town." Back in the days we could hear each other's thoughts and I did not want to articulate my question about that old man and was waiting for a reply. He said, "The press did not mention him but from the map of destruction, I would guess that he died." Then I went to my room and looked at the stick of amulet I was gifted from the old man and a tear rolled down my cheek. I kept it in my cupboard and life moved on. Then when I was seventeen, I had to go to Japan on a military mission and was stationed at a barrack in Japan. I slept their overnight and next day as I was walking out of there, I found an old man sweeping the floors. I walked past him and took a halt and turned around and walked slowly back to him and kneeled down and looked into his eyes. I stared for a whole minute before fully recognizing him. I then slowly asked him about his whereabouts. He could guess that I was from royalty even though I had a military suit. He mentioned the name of the same village and I didn't speak for another thirty seconds and said, "Do you remember that little boy who you gave the 'Aye-sokee'?" He did remember and started crying instead of speaking. I did not know how to express after that and started crying along with him. After few minutes of that, I raised him from there and took him to a nearby barrack and asked him about what all happened during that attack. I learnt that the comet took his house away and his entire family. He was away on a mission to Okiguawa. He was informed of the news a day later. When he went home, he saw his house was in collapsed state and charred bodies of his family lying around. He cried for hours and then cremated his family. Very little of the valuables were left unburnt. He gathered those and took off to a nearby town where some of his ancestors lived. He went on to living a meagre existence, just surviving by, doing menial work here and there till he took a janitorial job at that barrack. He asked about I had been. I talked about my life, in smaller bits because I kept thinking and planning about how I could help him out of his plight. I wanted to talk to my father about taking him home and giving him a job at the palace. Then I figured that my father would not approve that and moved on to finding ways of helping him within that region. So, I took him to a barrack where there were better standards of living for people and showed them my badge proving that I am the Korean king's son and asked them to get him the job of a cook which would be easier on his old age and more respected. I was able to get him that job after some altercation because they had a cook who needed to be placed elsewhere. This caused a delay of a day and a half, but my father wasn't too worried. I went home and tried a way of maintaining a connection with the old man. There was a way of keeping contact even ~1900 years ago using a version of the cell phone that was provided then by our star administration and confined to royalty. I got one made for him during that day and a half. It was hard for me to keep him at that job. Fist two weeks he had to tip toe and suffer more insult among the kitchen than his menial job for years. Though in his heart he felt someone cared for him and tried to do better so blamed it on destiny and even God. After that it was smoother because I was at my father's feet and asked him to call the Japanese king who called his administration at the barrack and asked that the old man's job be secure. Then after few months later, I was notified that he died. I was in the middle of a scientific mission. I took leave and hurried to Japan suspecting foul play. On my way I had to hurdle through barricades set up to block me. My suspicion was right. He was getting rebuked a lot at his job and was eventually beaten to death by the previous cook's family. I called the police and filed complaints and got all the five men that were involved in his murder, executed by hanging. This caused antagonism from the locals towards the Korean government and they filed a complaint to the then Japanese Emperor. The Emperor kind of chuckled about this and called my father and said, "You are losing your son to a homeless." And then sweet talked him into some political goodies that would please him. And then asked him to remove me from that case. Then I got a call from my father. He angrily asked me to return as soon as possible and report to him. I felt sad but the man was dead, and his killers died too, and he didn't have any relatives, so I retreated home. I went home and met my father. He looked at me with disapproval, fishing for my sentiments toward the Japanese old man, trying to find my level of attachment to him. He could perceive that I was very sad and angry about what had happened to the old man. He then went on to thinking how he could put me on a plan to revive my allegiance to himself.

Life went by for me. I never went to Japan after that. I was asked to go to Japan 35 years later for a political purpose. My son was king then of Korea and wanted me to talk to the ambassador. I refused to go because I had developed an emotional block against that place. My health deteriorated after that and I died six days later." I asked his people who were channeling, "Why did he die?" Someone said, "He was not useful."

KEEPING OUR KARMA UP

Almost all that we do and experience can be summarized as a mix of convergent and divergent actions of what we do and what is done to us, which eventually balances out over time following Newton's Laws of Motion stating that for every action there is an equal and opposite reaction. This is analogous to the laws of Karma.

The biggest teaching for keeping our Karma up is through the saying,

"God helps those who help themselves."

I happened to once watch a video by a famous motivational speaker. He spoke about shortcuts to succeeding in life and coming out a winner despite adversities. I was surprised at the messages because it seemed to be a summary of how I had been running my life until I arrived in the USA. The video talked about having an unfaltering intent to succeed continuously, overlooking roadblocks to your goals. During my developmental ages, I was always on my toes so that I could break the thick glass ceiling of my culture, my country and of poverty. Some of the precepts that I followed until I was twenty-four, was:

❖ Cruise through adversities with a strong intent to succeed, overlooking encumbrances in the surroundings.
❖ Don't include ruining other people for your own gain in the means to achieving your goals.
❖ Ignore people who pull you down, just not in action but also in feelings.
❖ Writing down your goals help. This acts as a personal reminder to us being steadfast and working hard towards succeeding.
❖ Keep trying as long as you think that the goals still make sense.
❖ Be vigilant of hindrances that could actually block you and take action preemptively.
❖ Relying on others is a recipe for failure.

I changed after I moved to the USA in 2002. I had slogged academically to be able to find an excellent job after graduating and accrued relevant credentials to be able to come to the USA on a full tuition waver, at a reputable college. However, life was much slower paced in Nashville, TN. After spending two years there, I took a job in Boston as a software developer. Boston was way different. I felt more alive. It reminded me of Calcutta where life is fast paced, and you can buy most things money can buy. My one year stay in Boston was the best time I had in my whole life. This was the first time I experienced freedom. On the first Friday evening, after arriving home from work, I realized that I didn't have a work-related task to complete. I remember that instead of being elated, I felt a slight panic. I didn't know what I could possibly do with that free time. I had the freedom to do "anything" with a whole weekend. It felt like I had time and money and did not know how to use them together. I slowly learnt to take time out for self-reflection. I didn't know much about the American culture, so I started watching a movie a day to catch up somewhat on the American culture. After a year I had completed watching seventy-three American movies.

In June 2005, I moved to Redmond, WA, after I took a job with a large software company. It has been thirteen years since then and my inspirational speech would be a lot different now if I had to give one. I guess life was incomparably more comfortable than how it was growing up, in terms of having a dishwasher to do my dishes, having a washer and a dryer to do my laundry, having a car to do my groceries and travel around, having money for amenities and having money to pay my mortgage and utility bills.

My motivational speech now, would go along the lines of:

❖ Live and let live.
❖ Do not be set back by failure.

❖ Sometimes, the divine has better things in store for you, so change is not always bad.

❖ If you pray, make sure, what you ask for doesn't hurt others and is within the boundaries of your karma and the destiny of your soul.

❖ Many people ask for more. It comes from greed or ignorance. Never serves in the long run. People only dig themselves a bigger hole till they arrive at a bottomless pit.

❖ Karma is a real thing. There are always inevitable consequences to actions.

❖ Acting from a place of compassion is not a recipe for failure. It opens our heart and mind and we are able to put in the other people's shoes.

❖ Taking time out for self-reflection is a good thing. It develops our right brain which in turn develops our left brain.

❖ Projection is a common human trait. People project their shortcomings unto others, sometimes in an accusatory way, and sometimes by wanting others to not succeed in what they find lacking within themselves.

❖ The judgers are not sent by the divine and they are struggling with their own desperation.

❖ Focus on how this life is going to pertain to your future lives.

After reading the above paragraph, a friend asked, "How do you feel now as a woman?"

Humanity has not broken itself away from the mold of not being able to accept women in leadership positions. I was content in my image and value as a woman. It is just that I learnt differently about some woman than the beliefs I used to hold. Deep inside they only alienate themselves farther from the core of their existence as a part of the divine feminine. These days I am still content in my being a woman and I do not wish to be a man at all. I find my mathematical and analytical brain to be no less competent than male brain. Accepting the existence of polarity and developing ourselves within our frame of who we are is the right investment of time and matter.

I experienced the worst of womanhood through my experiences in the last two years. In the beginning I just felt surprise and kept chugging along, hoping they would improve. I no longer feel like being a feminist. In past, I used to side with women who were raised meagerly in their developmental years whom society had shortchanged them in general. I always fought for their cause and lent my ears to their grievances and worked on solving those problems. I still stand up for the underdog and agonize at the sight of injustice.

Even in rich families, sometimes women are not treated with respect and not held accountable to the needs of achieving in society. I want women to start working for themselves. I encourage women to not wait for a man's approval to know their worth. Back-stabbing other women or playing the one-up game with other women would not get us far, collectively. I have had the honor of some men with tremendous political skills thinking that I have excellent oration skills and can convey political messages with grace. I take those compliments with regard but don't get carried away with it and neither judge nor compare with other women about those skills, and neither with men. I believe that each individual's soul comes with its own characteristics irrespective of gender which are built over the years through experience and the use of the innate talents and how they responded to their situations.

I want us to treat men and women equally in terms of bringing forth intelligent work in the form of Art and Science to humanity. Employers must work at bringing equality at the workplace. This will help reduce discrimination which begets deeper emotional problems, depression, and uncalled for stress injected into the work environment, which after prolonged periods of time leads to lower throughput from the discriminated person thus breeding the forebodings of the ones discriminating, resulting in a chicken and egg problem.

People who want to help others are good people, however providing undeserved help to someone is a spiritual crime because then we are messing with the larger divine hologram of justice for all. The light rewards hard work that is done within the parameters of justice. Hard work that is done to thwart justice is not rewarded, hence we find people who do that and bang their head thinking they are doing good but God or the divine in other words is not rewarding them in return.

Harboring sense of entitlement is a rising issue. There are people who expect good things to happen to them without working for it. We need to work for what we want to achieve.

Helping ourselves without stepping upon other people's foot brings good karma.

SEPARATING THOUGHT AND ACTION

Thinking poorly or even callously is benign, acting upon those thoughts isn't. We are accountable for our actions and it is our responsibility to discern our thoughts and inspect them to ascertain if they are legal, rational, socially acceptable, and going to bring justice to us and others before putting them into action. The biggest difference between a sage and someone working to achieve wisdom is acting upon all or most of our thoughts, versus analyzing our thoughts and consciously choosing to act or dismiss the thoughts that arise in our minds. I want to bring attention to the fact that just dismissing a thought is different from analyzing a thought for its validity, cause and repercussions if acted out. It is important to internalize the learnings of why we thought in a certain way and take corrective actions for a better life.

There are occasion when we use deviant thoughts to bring humor to self and others, but the purpose of such thoughts are purely to generate laughter which dispels more filth than a bit of what was created by the thoughts that may have been less than pure. For example, there are sitcoms that dig into the darker aspects of our existence to put people on the spot about the darker secrets of life and the more we connect, the more we laugh. There are usually two kinds of audience here, those who have committed such follies or their past thoughts match with the comical episode and so they laugh in agreement as if they have been caught red handed, and the other group of people who restrict themselves to only good thoughts, and so the episode triggers their minds to go through a circuitry that is considered perverted by them and so their minds find it a foray to venture out and laugh in rapture of the mind in the embarrassment of being caught delving into vicarious pleasure.

Spiritually, satire is a way of taking us through a path into the darker parts of our psyche, throwing light on them and releasing them through laughter. Laughter is equivalent to crying in releasing pent-up emotion. The process of laughter creates waveforms in the brain which passes through it in the form of beats and superpositions of sinusoidal waves. These are similar to waveforms that are created in the process of Sound Healing with the help of a tuning fork by the ear, or the ringing of a bell around the body to shed off energetic debris. These waves dislocate heavier energy and subsequently carry them away from the body.

Most sorts of comedy are good for our health, not just our physical health because our energy has gotten purer of heavier or darker thoughts which act like lumps or stiffness in the body but also for our emotional, and spiritual health which is also collectively cleansing for the Collective Consciousness.

There are teachings for ascension, such as self-reflection and observing other social rules which help us in keeping our karma up but the biggest practice that can really raise our own consciousness is not acting upon all our thoughts and segregating the thoughts for how reasonable and justified they are and only acting upon the ones that pass that bar. Separating thought and action is the fastest ladder to attaining Moksha, which is the goal of Buddhism and similar practices where ascending from the cycle of rebirth is important.

"Is it rude?", someone asked me in a classful of people learning about evolved thoughts and action. The context isn't important; it is rather repetitious.

"Truth is rude to negative people," I found myself replying.

I always feel bad for people who have been treated with injustice and never really point out other people's shortcomings or mistakes but sometimes we are forced to call them out to enforce the truth, to enforce justice and to bring in clarity, otherwise people take politeness for granted as a form of validation for their negative actions.

The flip side of not acting out most of our thoughts is that we think too much about too many what-ifs and so performing duediligence is good to discern how much we should sweep under the rug. So, voicing up and standing up for oneself is a good example of something we should act out more often rather than keeping it in our thoughts and festering it within ourselves.

THE REAL NATURAL HEALING: PSYCHOSOMATICS

Psyche is the Greek word for mind and 'soma' for the body. The reason I wanted to bring attention to this topic is because I wanted to lay down what the real natural healing is as opposed to alternative healing methodologies available to people such as naturopathy, acupuncture, energy healing, shamanic healing, spiritual healing, holistic healing, etc. Psychosomatic medicine pertains to the relationship between the mind and the body. The mind's thought is rewarded by the divine in the magnitude of power used and repetitions of it. Therefore, we can think ourselves into wellness or think ourselves into sickness.

We are designed to heal on our own without much medical intervention. When we get injured our body stores packets of information that tells what happened to that area in terms of mechanics of the injury with steps to heal. This gets stored in the muscle registry in a FIFO order. The fetching of the information and subsequent fixing is usually initiated through the process of yawning when the psyche is trying to heal the body. The yawning stretches the particular body parts in a particular way releasing the stored information needed for healing it optimally and sends it directly to the Somatic Nervous System. The Somatic Nervous System then takes action upon the stored message about our injury from which the body needs to recover. The stored information has very precise steps of unraveling the effects of the injury and does not include information about how we responded during the injury just about what happened to the body in terms of actions and damages. The information is stored at the location of the injury in a pouch-like invisible encasing, causing swelling. That is the main reason injury is associated with swelling. When we yawn, we release this information which gets carried to our central nervous system and very rapid action or fixing happens to address the injury. This includes myofascial release along with tendon realignment and muscle relaxation and adjustment of it to its right place. Sometimes the yawning process happens surreptitiously using Darkness powers or need to be externally induced with the use of technology from the stars or from the light. This happens very occasionally when the body refuses to heal up due to too many wounds or soul-parts wanting to die.

Psychosomatic healing is specifically useful for back issues where we have thinner muscles and so the information is stored nearer to the surface of the skin. The muscles there are woven into each other delicately. Hot or cold compression of the back leads to incorrect fixing which usually causes cascading issues in the adjoining areas. The recommendation is to let the body heal on its own. Even applying too much pressure messes with the stored information in the muscle lump at the site of injury. Softer massage and gentle strokes help the stored information to reach the central nervous system so that self-healing can happen. That's all is pretty much needed for sports injuries that does not include dislocated, broken or fractured bones.

Our medical treatment of injuries is sometimes in opposition to how they should be healed naturally. When injured, we are asked to put ice on the injured area. Ice compression evaporates away the information stored in the packets to bring right fixing for the particular injury. Even heat compression evaporates the information out. This occurs because the body's neurological system is very sensitive to heat and cold outside the range of normal tolerance. The Somatic receptors located in the injured area empty out because the temperature change ruins the neurological set of instructions that are like a microprocessor assembly instruction set waiting to be sent to the brain to fix the injury. Once the area is all iced up there is very little information left for the body to fix itself without undergoing external manipulation for which we rely upon educated estimates provided by x-rays or CT scans. These are good second-rate options but not as accurate as the supercomputer created by the divine which is our self-sustaining bodies. The divine light has genetic encoding of our existence and was created by the ultimate intelligence available.

When our injuries are not fully healed, the problem lingers until an adjoining area is injured and the information set for fixing that includes information for fixing the lingering issue for complete healing of the new injury. That's one reason why exercise and massage is a good thing because when we break scar tissues, the areas of the body where the scar tissues broke get a store of new information set for healing up.

Our physical body is coupled to our emotional body. The emotional body contains both positive energies of success and happiness and negative energies of experienced grief, repressed emotions and unresolved trauma. Energetically, the negative energies look like darker inanimate blocks or they are wounded soul-parts. When emotional injury occurs, the unprocessed emotions get stored in the Chakras associated with those functions as well as in the acupressure points for those types of wounding. What happens behind the scenes is that the parts of our whole selves that took the brunt of the injury or the grief, gets chunked off in a soul-part which dwells in that issues and is a wounded soul-part which is called a wound by the healers. This wound gets stored in the body at the assigned acupuncture point for those kinds of emotional trauma but that is not true if you have been spiritually because then they may move around the wounds. The location of the wound festers because that wounded soul parts grieves and produced toxic thoughts and spews out the negativity projected onto it. The wound feels stuck and mulls over its issues again and again and so over time the place in the body where the wound is located gets diseased.

These emotional wounds send signals to the brain which resemble a physical injury that has not occurred. Our brains cannot heal physical manifestations of emotional wounding such as lumps or stiffness in the body occurring from unprocessed emotional trauma, because the information packets from those sites, if they exist at all, don't provide details of how that lump or stiffness in the physical body came about. However, the divine had designed a not-so-direct way of healing emotional wounds naturally. Until about a 100,000 years ago, the brain tried to create outward circumstances to cause physical injuries to the person at the location of emotional wounding, so that the area can be fixed because the new set of psychosomatic information packets would have the steps of what all happened to the physical body so that those steps could be addressed for a full fixing of that region. It sounds sad but that is how our energetic makeup used to be, whereby the repeat injury used to be physical in order to generate the instruction set for the Somatic Nervous System for fixing that area.

About a 100,000 years ago the spiritual laws were changed to make the repeat wounds necessary for fixing physical conditions arising out of emotional wounding to be emotional wounds. For example, women who have had father issues growing up, finds a man in a relationship with whom the role and the wounding is replayed, on the other hand, for men if their mothers were demanding, their wives tend to treat them similarly. In this model, there is no net healing of emotional wounding, there is only piling up of further emotional wounds with no healing at all unless the person gets clairaudience and clairvoyance and starts healing their wounds spiritually or finds an Energy Healer who can heal their wounds and consequently the physical conditions created by those wounds. The repeat wounding type was switched from physical to emotional, to block us from living a long better life where people are happy past a certain age all the way to old age.

As it is evident by now, the natural process of healing works better in case of physical injuries and does not work too well in case of emotional injuries. Left untreated, the various types of wounds and griefs stored in the body lead to a coordinated physical response into shaping our body into visible expressions of sorrow, fear, anxiety, anger and guilt that is outwardly apparent as postures of grief, for example, hunched back, and frozen shoulders. Massage comes handy here because when we massage out the area where there are emotional wounds, the broken tissues carry information packets that are useful in somewhat healing that area naturally.

Someone wanted to know if going to a psychologist or a psychiatrist is useful in healing emotional wounds. They don't talk to the wounds directly like how the Energy healers do but when the psychiatrist explains and talks through their situation the wounds hear and develop understanding of their problems and feel better progressively. As a wounded soul-part starts feeling better they aren't producing further grief energy anymore and so their surrounding negative energies get slowly handled by the lymphatic drainage as well as through the natural process of elimination of toxins. In summary, there is benefit in seeing a psychiatrist though the recovery is slower than how the wounds get healed when we are working with them spiritually.

COLOR THERAPY

Using the color analogy, our energy is made of a combination of wavelengths of light. Deficiencies of certain wavelengths cause diseases because it is aberration from our original blueprint signature. Placing colors that are deficient for our makeup close to our body transmits that color in a scatter effect to our energy system. It is best to place the color in the region where that color is deficient or had been reduced due to disease or other forms of spiritual attacks.

Human bodies have seven chakras. Sages also have only seven chakras. They get an additional chakra conferred upon them by our star administration, so that they could draw greater power from the divine and the relics from certain benign light realms to channel it for healing purposes to other people and pets.

The colors of the seven chakras are Red for the bottom most root chakra governing the legs and grounds us on earth, Orange for the sacral chakra governing the genitals, Yellow for the solar plexus chakra representing personal power, Green for the heart chakra representing compassion, love and beauty, Blue for the throat chakra representing ability to communicate, Indigo for the third eye which is the seat of clairvoyance and Violet for the crown chakra which connects us to the Universe.

The chakra system contains the seven chakras and smaller energy centers very much like the neurological system flowing through the body carrying messages between the motor nerves and the sensor nerves causing and controlling mobility and function of the involuntary muscles. Keeping the chakras clear helps in keeping a clearer energy body resulting into good health physically, mentally, emotionally and spiritually.

We can raise our vibration through infusing colors that have higher vibrations such as the neon colors. Raising our own vibration helps us in feeling higher states of bliss and a general happiness and feelings of fulfillment.

Synergistic healing through Color Therapy is also achieved using relics that have been pre-programmed to feed various lights through the different layers of our body to cure a disease or achieve an overall healthier end result for ourselves.

The Reiki healing rays are rays of the Castor star. This is usually for Korean people and the sun belong to the star administration of Korean people. Reiki was popularized in America by the Japanese who are about one third Korean in origin.

The mechanisms of working of Reiki, is that light from a certain star was directed to people through someone attuned for it. Light has certain spectrum and certain frequencies. Each of the colors or wavelengths of that Light had different effectiveness in curing different diseases. These colors are used individually or in particular mix for patients.

The biggest difference between Color Therapy and Energy Healing is that most of the work done in Energy healing is localized and Color Therapy can address the entire body at once including all four aspects of the body , mental, physical, spiritual and emotional.

MAKING OURSELVES WHOLE

When we suffer from a loss, a trauma or meet with an accident, or if we suffer through emotional issues over prolonged periods of time, parts of ourselves that could not agree with or tolerate such experiences leave the body resulting in soul loss and the parts of the whole that have left are called soul-parts. The soul-parts that leave under traumatic situations are the ones that:

❖ Could not agree with the negative experience.
  o An example would be the loss of the ability to trust in case of deceit from a trusted someone who had knowingly led them into a preplanned torture or a harrowing experience.
❖ Could not tolerate that experience.
  o This usually happens in the case of extreme trauma such as a car accident, extreme torture,

drowning, burning etc. The parts that usually leave are the gifts and qualities that could not linger through the nature of the experience and goes against the definition of what the spiritual makeup should be at some point through the trauma, such as the 'will' in case of a prolonged torture.

❖ Couldn't fight back.

  o Usually the soul-parts that are lost are along the lines of the ability to fight back such as in a prolonged struggle through being beaten to death if it stretched over more than an hour.

❖ Come to terms with that state of existence.

  o This usually happens as a slow process, for example, in the case of jail convicts who exhibit some hope for the first few months whether they had committed that crime or not, and then parts of them that couldn't come to terms with that experience leave. In this case, the soul-parts that are usually lost are to do with the ability to receive love, happiness, cheerfulness, ability to express emotionally, etc.

The human body is like a bag of mix of soul energy of one or more types and comprise of various qualities such as the gifts or skills of happiness, will, perseverance, being able to receive love, being able to give love, skills of wizardry, self-love, ability to trust others, ability to be comfortable with power, ability to stand up for self, ability to fight back and so on. Humans do know about soul loss intuitively, as proven by occasions when they feel or say,

"I was never the same again."

"I lost a part of me."

"I felt empty."

"My heat broke."

We intuitively want to recover from soul loss. Examples of such feelings are,

"I want to pick myself up."

"Pull oneself together."

"I need to put myself back together."

"I want to become whole again."

Energy healers and Shamans help us by retrieving our soul-parts and healing them if they are wounds and integrating them in our bodies. Soul retrieval is a process of journeying into the hidden invisible realms of Earth and recovering the lost soul parts and integrating them into the body.

Wounds are formed when the wounded fragment of our whole self, get compartmentalized into a state of existence where they think that the atrocity that happened upon them, or the pain they experienced is still happening perpetually unless rescued and healed with love, compassion and counselling.

These wounds are like a bite out of an apple where the apple is the whole self. However, that bite doesn't look or feel like a bite but another apple itself and feels, acts, talks and thinks like the whole self with the gifts and attributes of only that part of the soul. So, our whole self is mix of qualities and talents. When a part is chunked off it has its own talents and qualities which are usually missing from the rest of the self, depending on how much of those qualities or talents existed in the whole self. In summary, wounds are soul-parts that are in a wounded rut and don't feel well until healed.

Shamans heal the wounds by showering them with compassion and talking to them about their issues like a psychotherapist would do. We can't talk to our wounds or soul-parts unless we have clairaudience or clairvoyance. It takes a few weeks to heal a wound. The healing ability depends upon the healer's power of channeling divine light and the healer's closeness to the divine nature.

The soul parts need a continuous transmission of healing energy for about 20 to 30 minutes, after which psychotherapy is required to draw them out of their traumatic states and make them feel accepted. They need care and nurturance to be brought from the shadows into accountability and acceptability. After the wounds start feeling normal they get integrated into our whole selves and become part of our lives, expressing their qualities through the physical body.

I want to bring attention to the fact that crying helps heal the emotional body. Crying is a healing outlet enabling the body to release pent-up emotion from the body that was stored earlier as a result of an unprocessed grief. On a later time when the unprocessed grief is accessed via a similar situation or a repeat incident or by divine touch or being in touch with compassionate energy and it is shallow enough that it can come up to the surface the emotions are released in the form of tears and processed out to lighter energy within our body bringing in healing. However, some of the emotions are very buried deep within the core of us and quite hardened due to the intensity of the torture. Those are brought to the surface only via psychological talking. This is why we have psychologists for resolving old trauma from childhood and other longstanding, repressed grief.

Integrating unhealed wounds is possible, but they won't spread out into the whole body and would remain in a particular place like a lump and feel like a stiffness. Also, if the wounds are left unhealed, they entrench the body in their sorrow or the particular issue about which they were wounded as such as fear of a particular disease, fear of success, fear of failure, beliefs of unworthiness, guilt about something, or wounding from physical or emotional trauma.

The unhealed wounds are hooks for others to latch onto, eventually bringing in life's unfair dues. The wounds also think, and thoughts influence what the body experiences, for example, when a person has a wound stemming from lack of love, they cannot receive love in their lives because the complications of the wound get projected onto a pattern, blocking fulfillment in that area.

Unless the above knowledge reaches people, or they get spiritual teaching from a healer who could help to integrate them into a whole, they might not know in their waking consciousness about the needs of mending the fragmented self.

Photo taken at the main square at Kathmandu, Nepal.

ENERGY HEALING FOR RESETTING OUR BODIES

Natural healing through prayer, spirituality, herbs and divinity used to be the norm in ancient times. Over time, we have weaned ourselves away from our true, spiritual selves.

Spiritual healing is a real thing; our solid bodies are really condensed energies, and everyone have their own true blueprint signature energy that governs the physical body's structure and functioning. Our Charkas are the hubs of the electronic circuitry that makes up the body, with the Acupuncture points mapping on to the Chakra system. Thus, we are energy woven in a certain configuration to make up our bodies.

Spirit just means etheric or energetic form of a soul and spirituality just means believing in the existence and knowledge of our energetic or spirit form.

Energy healing constitutes bringing positive energy and removing negative energy to achieve a certain result and may also employ Shamanic work which employs a lot of native spirits, mountains, trees and nature-spirits and is more earth-based. Korean shamans in antiquity healed a lot of the ailments using all sorts of Earth based techniques and rays of the Sun. The spirit of a dead, Mongolian Shaman who lives in the East, which is a shamanic concept of Middle World Directions, occasionally helps me in my healing work.

During the process of energy healing, relevant good energy is added through a process which is like an infusion, and foreign and disease energies are removed by a process of extraction which feels in the body like dissipating energy out.

People have benefited from spiritual healing in all areas of life including mental fogging, physical and emotional issues such as anxiety, depression, lack of mental focus, bone and joint issues, TMJ (temperomandibular joint) disease, digestion problems including IBS (irritable bowel syndrome), inability to attract a desired life partner, issues with loss and coping, feeling stuck in life and not knowing their calling or purpose in life, issues from childhood abuse and other forms of trauma.

The reason removal of misplaced energy from our body helps is because the foreign energy acts against the true, blueprint signature energy of ours, much like when physical foreign objects are in the body, the body triggers an immune reaction recruiting cells, causing inflammation. Additionally, when the foreign energy has emotional charge, it serves as a lens or prejudice with which we experience the world. After that energy is cleared, we don't see the world through that lens anymore and we don't project it into our relationships through that intrusion or thoughtform. Usually about seventy percent of the foreign energy is in the form of a consciousness that talks and feels in a certain way much like a soul and rest are inanimate energy or noise representing a certain thoughtform or hologram. After we have cleared the congestive energy from all four of our energy bodies, we begin to know our true selves.

There are four aspects to our energetic existence. The physical that you can touch, the spiritual which is the soul that leaves at the time of death, the emotional which is stored in various parts of the body specially at the acupuncture points and not just in the head, and the mental part which is the brain and the entire nervous system governing our thoughts, actions and reactions. These four types of bodies act in a synchronized mode, and feed into each other like a Control System feedback loop.

There are healing modalities that use the four energy bodies synergistically to heal the whole self usually through Color therapy. Synergistic healing is also possible by sending sound vibration through the body. Examples of such healing are Qi Gong, and even playing musical instruments, singing aloud, ringing bells and chimes over the body to dislocate heavy energy and releasing them. Singing aloud in the shower is especially useful because water acts as a medium to carry away the heavier energies out of the body.

I am going to talk about our Body Aspect which is a divine part of ourselves catering to our physical needs and keeping us alive, warning us continuously of any imminent danger and has its own divine mechanisms of veering us away from bodily harm. The body is usually the last to react. There is reason for this. The powers of darkness work in the presence of it such as facing something or someone directly or touching the energy within the reach of it, so unless we are face-to-face where we can see or physically touch the energy it is harder to fathom using darkness powers. For darkness, "seeing is believing" is more accurate than for the light powers. Other than that, elemental powers also work when you are directly invoking it in sight or within perception. We usually perceive danger way before it is in sight, by means of being connected to the light from where our seeds are. Someone asked to explain why. This is because light travels a whole lot faster than sound does, and darkness and elemental energy is of the constitution of about five times denser than audible sound frequencies on Earth.

Healing sessions that I offer include divination about the most important healing needed as well as any specific problems you may want to work on. Energy work that is done is soul retrieval, removal of lumps and stiffness from the body that are blocks of your own energy representative of emotional wounding and grief, and foreign blocks of energies not belonging to you such as dead people, curses, intrusion and disease energy. It also includes past life and ancestral healing. After a healing session, salt bath is recommended with saltiness close to the levels of the ocean waters. This would help purge and readjust your body easily to the healed energy blueprint, with less fatigue.

I mentioned in the previous chapter that people could use wound healing. This becomes more important once the number of wounds accumulate to more than forty. Statistically, the average American accumulates forty wounds by the age of thirty-one. The energy healers locate the wounded soul-parts, cleans up the accumulated "hoocha" or dense energies around them, take them out of their place of hiding or wherever in the body they live and shower them with compassion and do talk therapy like a psychiatrist to bring them out of their traumatic state and help them with acceptance and healing, and then eventually integrate them into the whole body.

Energy healing is needed to achieve justice from how the wounds are designed to accumulate over time after the negative reforms in the spiritual laws a 100,000 years ago. Also, when people have misunderstandings, they inadvertently send undue curses and some people who are a perverted witch, or a sorcerer would knowingly send negative energies to good people and steal off their good karma. It is like the speed remedy for the need to go to a psychiatrist or an acupuncturist.

I had temporomandibular joint dysfunction popularly known as TMJ for more than thirty-three years, which was healed in one go when the energy causing the dislocation was removed by a Shaman. The energy causing the dislocation was a solidified, dead tree refuse material that happened to be in that position.

In another example, in the month of June 2016, one morning I noticed that my right knee was almost crippled and I could not walk properly. I couldn't tell what was wrong and by then I used to talk to spirits already so kept asking for spiritual help to get my knee fixed. I noticed that a tendon in the right leg was detached and kicked out of its position near the knee. The femur was also rotated abnormally and slightly dislocated out of the acetabulum at the hip. Several sacroiliac ligaments were stretched out and the major tendon connecting the two sides of the acetabulum was rotated and slightly dislocated out of place. After two and a half weeks of living in agony, one morning, as I was about to wake up, I felt that someone twisted my hip back to position and set the knee tendon back to its position. After that the dislocation was gone but the inflammatory damage to the cartilaginous tissue loss took time to heal.

Some of the sports injury can be fixed by spiritual laser surgery. This is achieved by projecting and passing light beams of varying wavelength in conjunction with the invisible probes and tools which are constructed out of elemental, darkness and light powers to move things around just like our physicians use their hands, probes, and other tools. Swelling from injury can be healed spiritually using sound and alchemy, just like the physicians use therapeutic, ultrasound on the swollen areas of the body. However, surgery requiring forceful adjustments are not always possible because the human reality is different from the spiritual reality and the tactile forces have to go through a barrier which could work if we leveraged the lever mechanics but normally we don't, given we have medical facilities in our physical human reality and that would like sacrificing a bull for minimal gains. All kinds of non-invasive surgery are not possible spiritually, because our realm is different from theirs, which is way less dense than ours, so by the laws of Physics:

$$force = mass * acceleration, \text{ and}$$

$$mass = density * volume,$$

Hence the force applied upon our body is too little because of their average density being a one-millionth to one-billionth of our bodies and instruments. That is why for a must do spiritual surgery which isn't possible using spiritual probes, lever mechanics employing a whole planet or a star's powers is used.

Some of the other uses of energy healing is house or office inaugural clearing, when the space is cleared of imprints of trauma, unwanted energy and general healing of the environment. Spirits are attached to a place for various reasons which need to be addressed with compassion and cleared. These could be fairies who do exit, dead people, dead dogs and even nature sprites.

What we can gain from a hundred-dollar energy healing session, would traditionally take thousands of dollars and much longer recovery time than the work from a spiritual healing session. Many kinds of surgeries can be done using laser beams and the laser beams are from the Light or from some of the stars depending upon the specific case. Examples of laser surgeries that can be done upon us are optical vision correction, bone joint surgery, vasectomy, removal of cancerous cells, easement of childbirth, plastic surgery of all kinds, neurosurgery and ortho-dontic work.

It is important to receive energy healing from a person of higher vibration because they can channel light which isn't laced with negative energies. Also, the lighter ones' energy gets the easier it is for them to heal themselves more and raise their vi-bration. Denser energies keep us low and the healer needs to be shining their own light before they can heal others. This is one reason why to some people, "shaman" brings up the image of a quack, who would do you Abracadabra and run with your money.

In the past, Stars like Arborra and Obalesk have helped heal diseases and raise frequency of human bodies and Earth, and I am here to help with that. This work would help us heal, attain more wisdom and compassion, and collectively help us realize the full potential of our souls.

On the topic of choosing an energy healer, spiritual healing is like a big club too where there are people looking for different kinds of remuneration, and there is hierarchy and credibility of the living and the dead involved. Healers are chosen by the di-vine based upon their piety levels and connections. The abilities of channeling divine light is important for a healer and also their hierarchy in Darkness realms which run in an order of allegiance.

Complementary healing is also useful in cleaning our chakras and energy system. These are measures such as grounding, exercise and reading to learn from other people's mistakes and get ourselves self-therapy. Spending time in Ocean heals a lot of the ailments especially skin conditions due to the saltiness and the minerals in it. The Red Sea is well-known as a place for purging ourselves of negative and heavy energies that can be shed without the intervention of an energy healer or talk therapy.

Many people want to know what actually happens in an energy healing session. To give perspective of what happens I thought I would paste my testimonials from my energy sessions because they come from people availing themselves of energy healing and who do not know much about what goes on underneath the layers. The following testimonials from my healing sessions recount people's experiences through the sessions and how they felt about it afterwards.

"I went into the session with a heavy weight on my chest and on my head. About halfway through the session I could feel my weights being lifted... I went on to have multiple incidents of tingling throughout my body and strong tingling in my legs. At the end of the session my body continued to tingle all over. I felt more at peace and the heavy pressure I had felt was relieved. It was an invaluable experience full of calm and peace. I am thankful to Sarita Gupta for the clarity and calm she was able to provide me."

-   Name withheld, Seattle, WA.

"As soon as Sarita started rattling, I felt some energy rising inside me, it was easy to sit upright as something was pulling up, then this feeling almost disappeared. At some point I felt like the energy was spinning inside me, I got an urge to turn my head side to side to stretch the neck muscles. At the end of the session it got really interesting and comforting feeling like as if I was wrapped in soft, warm and cozy blanket. After the session, I felt…. It's strange to say…but more confident. It seems to be easier to focus and my thoughts cleared up a bit. It's already been a few days after the session, and I really hope this condition will stay long. Thank you so much."

-   Name withheld, Seattle, WA.

"The first day I met you, my intuition told me that spending time with you would help me to dissolve negativity. Since then, I have come to know you as someone who is intelligent, driven, ambitious, artistic, and giving. More importantly, there is something very unique about your energy. It is hard to put into words, it's something I had to feel to believe. Spending time with you has placed me on a journey of healing that has resulted in less anger and less brain fog. Every day that I see you, I feel less defeated and more empowered. I now feel joy when I wake up in the morning, and that is something that has not happened to me before. Thank you for helping me to forgive myself for my past mistakes. I look forward to continuing this journey with her."

- Name withheld, Redmond, WA.

"I am grateful to be working with Sarita to help clear out old patterns and beliefs and shift my energy and focus. I'm new to energy healing and am loving the results that I am seeing. Through energy healing sessions I am able to remove blocks, heal old wounds, and feel much lighter."

- Name withheld, Los Angeles, CA.

"I have worked with Sarita to get healing for myself. I found her committed and determined to do what was best for me. She has a wide range of knowledge and takes from different schools of shamanism and energy medicine. I would recommend her wholeheartedly."

-Name withheld, London, UK.

HOPE IS THE BEST MEDICINE WE NEED

Will prayer help me to get healed?

"Yes, prayer and setting intention works and will help you heal according to your prayer or intention. However, in cases where one is spiritually afflicted, for significant and rapid improvements, appropriate human intervention, is needed and that is where my spiritual knowledge and experience and divine relationships can help."

The combative one step up tendencies actually gets you one step down with each step with whoever you are playing the game with. Think of it like the morality game of Chutes and Ladders where the one-up tendencies with the opponent are the snakes that slide into evil and when both parties keep doing that instead of rising up, they both keep falling down one after another in succession. However, when one player takes the high road and shows peaceful compromise between themselves it brings the ladders of good acts thus climbing higher and encouraging the other party to follow the example and act similarly to borrow the ladder to rise higher.

I met a monarchal queen of a star somewhere in an invisible realm on Earth. On the topic of finding the right man to marry, she said, "Marriage happens between own type of people, with other type of people only mergers happen." She said that in the Hindi language where it sounds harsher and mean more like people should try to find marriage partners among their own type else it would not be a marriage but just an understanding to abide by for life and almost walk on eggshells to make it work. The purpose of this revelation is that on Earth people are not allowed to marry their own star origin type, to promote an environment for a more rapid growth spiritually through lessons and learnings. The saying that "Marriages are made in heaven." is not wrong. In the stars people marry almost the same person life over life for up to millions of lives or more. It is like having a "Life partner over lives." They plan to be born together and die together. While on Earth, the pairing is enforced by Earth's Darkness and even the Light relics for Earth which has the encoding for Earth's spiritual laws. The spiritual laws in Darkness says that the marriage partners can only have a body and soul Chemistry of twenty percent to sixty percent. In the testing situation that we are married to someone of having different likes and dislikes with whom we don't have much in common, we get hurled into an unknown situation from the get-go, which in the event of expected disagreements necessitates taking the high road to bring in harmony and understanding. The high road is analogous to faking it till we make it.

Hope is the best medicine we need. It cures diseases, the scientific explanation of which is that the positive thought attracts positivity which brings in positive healing energy to heal us. One step towards keeping hope is acceptance, which does not mean condoning the negativity around us but surrendering to the bigger scheme of the universe and looking forward to receiving justice and positive things in life. It is easier said than done because developing acceptance is a slow process but keeping hope to bounce back somehow helps because then we start seeing pathways that could build ourselves up and so it is easier to adhere to that understanding of acceptance and surrender. Without hope, over time, we lose the ability to receive, happiness, cheerfulness, ability to express emotionally, etc. When we are feeling really low, darkness may start seeming attractive. We originated from the light, so darkness doesn't really work for us which becomes evident rather quickly.

WORK NEEDED TO SAVE EARTH

Humanity's awakening is destined by the Divine and it is time that we get in touch with who we are, our destiny and our potential. However, a lot of work needs to be done for life to sustain on Earth and humanity to continue into bearing future generations of healthy children. However, humanity cannot fully clean up the invisible litter or solve some of the major problems which needs to be solved by the star benefactors of Earth.

The benevolent star people place chips in relevant scientists' heads so that they can hear them and cooperate into fixing certain problems of Earth. These are usually astronomers, astrophysicists, technicians of nuclear reactors, and other high-ranking officials.

Major fixing needs to happen in the Geophysics of Earth, the matter of the atmospheric layers and its depleted Ozone layer, the genome of humans, plants and the animal world and in the configurations of nearby planets and stars. There is a lot of work to be done to stabilize the magma core of the Earth and the Stratosphere. I hope we will begin to believe in all that this book has to say and be respectful of star people and other supernaturals.

Some of the examples of star people working together with us, are the measures taken to save ourselves from flooding.

❖ Flocculation was used to coagulate water in the Pacific Ocean so that Japan doesn't drown. This was done by using technology from the Andromeda galaxy. They used strong laser beams of churning device to churn the large mass of water. The powers used were from their stars and the light. The churning process increases the size of the water molecules, as a result of particle collision. This is because the centrifugal forces resulting from the churning motion, as well as the molecular collisions, distort the orbits of the electrons around the nuclei of water molecules causing formation of aggregates that pull inward exhibiting the effects of increased coagulation.

❖ Coagulants were added into water of certain bays to save adjoining lands. Some of these coagulants came from the Cetus galaxy. This is a temporary measure because it effects water quality but better than loss of lives and properties.

The hope is that the recent star-wars will end and that Earth's tilt, configuration of rotation and revolution of Earth and the properties of the magnetic core and its distance from the

Moon would be restored and so the threats of flooding can become minimal. The above temporary measures will then be reviewed and addressed.

Work is needed to squelch the Time machines working against Earth. 2012 was designed and geared to be real. The Time Machine was designed to explode Earth on the 30th of November of 2012, but the Hathors worked hard into messing with many Convergence Series in various pieces of the program for the process to not conclude into explosion. Even though we are well past it, the Time Machines need to be dismantled for the threats to fully go away. Right now, they are only partially damaged whereby the mathematical algorithms have been tweaked to buy time.

We have limited time if we do not wake up to the clarion call which our cognitive minds don't hear. It is our unintegrated soul parts that mostly live in non-ordinary reality, who interact with star people or get out of Earth and go wandering about places, some of which we are aware through our dreams as well as the 'non-dreams' which have I talked about in the chapter on "Dreams". So unless this broadcast reaches the masses and our soul parts also read it or people get spiritual healing from me or similar practitioners who could integrate our fragmented selves into whole, we would not know in our waking consciousness if we are under a war and if there are rules to follow and who we are, the root causes of our bigger problems and that we coexist with other humanoids in Space. The good news is that some of our soul parts can read what our bodies can read but they aren't always in the body and usually out and about for 10 percent of the times, in times of peace and 95% of times, in times of war. They can't turn pages of our book, but they can read what is in view.

EPILOGUE

I learnt that the books that humanity get to read are quite streamlined by the invisible people. The books are certainly not a product of pouring down from our hearts and minds on a piece of paper and publishing. I learnt that when someone's book is about to be published, they get approached by invisible people, some of who want to be heard, some of who want to judge and some of who are just mischief mongers, and some of who want to censor the contents. The authors who do not have clairaudience or clairvoyance are unaware of it cognitively, and unaware of the entire politics from the Outer Space going into what you can publish and what you cannot.

I learnt that certain soul-parts of the authors are taken to the light realms where they are celebrated as authors and people who have done charitable work for humanity because the books are cheaper than the effort that goes into it, costing as much as a meal. Some authors are taken to Darkness.

What happens to such people thereafter would be taking us away from the hope we need to keep ourselves afloat. Hope works.

BIOBLIOGRAPHY

1. Koscik, T.R.; Tranel, D. (2011). "The human amygdala is nec-essary for developing and expressing normal interpersonal trust". *Neuropsychologia.* **49** (4): 602-611. doi:10.1016/j.neuro-psychologia.2010.09.023. PMC 3056169.PMID 20920512.

2. Johnson, Horton A. "Teilhard's Convergence Principle." *Perspectives in Biology and Medicine, v*ol. 8, no. 3, 1965, pp. 394-402. Project MUSE, doi:10.1353/pbm.1965.0040

3. Bruce Shelley (April 9, 2007). "Play Age of Empires –Study History in College" Ensemble Studios. Archived from the original on February 17, 2008.

4. Quake (game manual). ID Software. 1996.

5. "2014 Annual Report" (PDF). Office of Historic Preservation, California State Parks, for "Mystery Spot".

6. Journal reference: *Nature Physics,* DOI: 10.1038/nphys3810 by Emmanuel Fort, Mathias Fink, and Antonin Eddi.

7. Reverso translation engine at https://context.reverso.net/translation/englishfrench/aspies for the word "Aspie".

8. "Toxic black snow covers Siberian coal mining region", The Guardian News and Media limited. Dated – 2/15/2019.

9.   Apple iphone Dictionary. "Solid State".

10. Britannica for the definition of Determinism. url: https://
www.britannica.com/topic/determinism. Last accessed March 2019.

11. Lauren Said-Moorhouse, CNN Published 9:22 AM EST, Sun,
December, News at https://www.cnn.com/2017/12/17/americas/
chile-landslideintl/index.html

12. Magnitude 7.8, Mon, Nov 14 2016, 12:02:56 am (NZDT)".
GeoNet. Retrieved November 12, 2018.

13. News at https://www.cnn.com/2017/12/17/americas/
chilelandslide-intl/index.html

14. 15 March 2018 landslide near Cusco, Peru. Galeria del
Ministerio deDefensa del Perú. Date - 15 March 2018, 15:28:37.
Source -https:// www.flickr.com/photos/
ministeriodedefensaperu/39935939755/in/dateposted/

Made in the USA
Columbia, SC
16 February 2023

12156254R00152